ALSO BY PAULA DRANOV

HEART DISEASE
A Random House Personal Medical Handbook

DIABETES
A Random House Personal Medical Handbook

FIRST AID
A Random House Personal Medical Handbook

ALLERGIES

▼

**A RANDOM HOUSE
PERSONAL
MEDICAL
HANDBOOK**

* Assistant professor of pediatrics, Johns Hopkins Hospital; recipient of the Harriet Lane Fellowship Award, Stetler Fellowship Award for Women Physicians, and Geigy Award for Clinical Research, American College of Allergists; and author of numerous publications and abstracts.

ALLERGIES

A RANDOM HOUSE
PERSONAL
MEDICAL
HANDBOOK

PAULA DRANOV

WITH A FOREWORD BY
JAN BERNHISEL-BROADBENT, M.D.*

RANDOM HOUSE
NEW YORK

Library of Congress Cataloging-in-Publication Data
Dranov, Paula.
Allergies: a Random House personal medical handbook
by Paula Dranov.
p.   cm.   —(A Random House personal medical handbook)
ISBN 0-679-72910-0
1. Allergy—Popular works.   2. Allergy—Handbooks, manuals,
etc.
I. Title.   II. Series.
RC584.D69   1990
616.97—dc20   90-8593
Designed by Beth Tondreau Design/Jane Treuhaft
Manufactured in the United States of America
2   4   6   8   9   7   5   3
First Edition

FOREWORD

▼

One out of every four to five people suffers from an allergic disorder, yet misinformation about allergy and allergic diseases abounds. The diversity and varied severity of allergic disease is fascinating. Why the same basic allergic mechanism leads to the nuisance symptoms of hay fever in one patient and life-threatening episodes of anaphylaxis in another is unclear. However, despite the numerous mysteries of allergy as yet unsolved, there is a wealth of information that anyone with a chronic allergic condition should be familiar with. This handbook is ideally suited to help people with allergies or families with allergic members achieve this goal. It provides easily understandable insight into the mechanisms responsible for allergy and in-depth discussions of specific allergic disorders, while dispelling much of the myths that exist on the subject. It also contains information that could be life-saving for people with severe allergies. Understanding the mechanisms, causes, and treatment options of allergic disease will help you and your physician to best manage your specific allergic problems.

One of the many highlights of this handbook is the

section containing the description of and treatment for anaphylaxis, and the emergency management of a severe allergic reaction. Unfortunately, it is still common for patients, families, and care givers to underestimate the potential severity and consequences of an accidental food or drug ingestion, insect sting, or unremitting asthma attack. Near-fatal or fatal anaphylactic episodes have a recurrent theme: delay in the administration of epinephrine and/or the refusal to seek immediate emergency treatment. This handbook clearly outlines how to be prepared in the event of a severe allergic reaction, how to recognize the signs and symptoms of a life-threatening allergic event, and the steps to take once a severe reaction has begun. One might argue that this planning effort places too much focus on disease, but I would argue that if you are well prepared, and if friends, family, and care givers are well informed, you can better relax and your disease will interfere less with your life.

The handbook is well balanced in its discussion of allergic diseases such as asthma, allergic rhinitis, and allergic eczema or atopic dermatitis. Avoidance precautions for potential allergens and disease-prevention measures are given a well-deserved emphasis. In addition, the indications for the use of medications and immunotherapy are clearly and concisely detailed.

Numerous people incorrectly believe that they have had an allergic drug reaction, insect sting, or food ingestion, when in fact they have had an expectable side-effect: nausea or diarrhea from an antibiotic; a large local reaction from a honeybee sting with no increased risk of systemic reaction; or bloating from milk due to a problem digesting lactose, rather than a true allergy to milk proteins. Accurate interpretation of what is and what isn't an allergic reaction, as well as treatment and management plans, can greatly affect your life-style. The topics of insect, drug, and food allergy are often surrounded by misinformation and confusion, and are greatly clarified by chapters in this handbook.

You will also find an informative discussion of common but unproven approaches to the diagnosis and treatment of allergic disorders. Those suffering from a frustrating or chronic illness, or desperate for a cure for headaches, depression, behavioral problems, or myriad other problems of their own or of family members may be enticed by claims that these are due to allergies, and embark on a course of attempted cure by these controversial approaches. These methods often require extensive alteration in life-style and are not all without harm. I have cared for patients with severe nutritional deficiencies secondary to medically unnecessary restriction diets of a degree typically seen only in third world countries.

The back of the book contains a remarkable resource list, appendix and glossary, which provide easily referenced information to enhance your understanding and care of allergies. This information can help you bridge the gap when dealing with unfamiliar medical terms, help you in finding a camp for your child with asthma, and even help you obtain a good price on a peak-flow meter to monitor your asthma The contents of this handbook with its provision for rapid reference of important information, together with the expertise of your physician and health-care providers, should enhance your understanding and make living with an allergic disorder easier.

JAN B. BROADBENT, M.D.

CONTENTS
▼

INTRODUCTION

▼

If you have an allergy, you already know that it is unlikely to seriously impair your health. But you may be coming to realize that, at the very least, it is an inconvenient and frustrating disorder. You may have to worry only part of the year, during hay-fever season. Or you may have an allergy that is always with you and requires you to watch what you eat or do battle with such unseen menaces as dust mites or mold spores. The severely allergic must maintain constant vigilance against substances that can set off a life-threatening emergency.

In the vast majority of cases, allergies can be controlled. This book is intended to help you with that task. Slip it into your pocket, purse or glove compartment, and take it with you everywhere as a ready source of information. Part diary, part reference book, it provides space to keep track of your allergy symptoms so you can identify and avoid the substances and circumstances that trigger them. Although written as a guide for patients, it is also an important resource for family members and friends. In the event of an emergency, you will probably need help: someone to call the doctor, drive you to the hospital or administer epinephrine if needed to quell a severe allergic reaction. Ask your spouse, a close friend and, definitely, a traveling companion to become familar with the book and its contents and know where to find it should an emergency arise.

The pages that follow are for use as a diary. They have been designed to enable you to keep track of any symptoms you experience, to record what you've been eating and what drugs you have been taking. Since some allergy symptoms, including asthma attacks, are triggered or worsened by strenuous physical activity, there are also pages to note how exercise affects you.

The diary section includes several pages for use as a record of any drugs you may be taking, the correct dosage, directions for use, potential side effects. There is room to note symptoms that could be drug-related.

Just beyond the diary pages, you'll find a section on emergencies. Place a paper clip or marker on the first page so you can turn to it easily. And be sure to ask family members, friends, traveling companions, teachers, trainers, coaches, to read it so they can recognize symptoms of a developing emergency and act appropriately.

In addition to the diaries, you will find chapters explaining what allergies and allergy symptoms are and what they are not. Individual chapters describe the various types of allergy; hay fever and similar conditions affecting the nose and eyes; asthma; allergies to foods, drugs, insect stings; and allergies affecting the skin. You also will find discussions of testing and treatment methods and their limitations.

Whatever it is, this book is not a substitute for your

doctor. It is not intended to second-guess your treatment or raise doubts about the quality of your medical care. No book can be all things to all patients. Individuals differ, and treatment must be individually tailored. If you have any questions about any aspect of your treatment as a result of information in this book, discuss your concerns with your doctor. Don't make any changes in your allergy or asthma medication without your physician's knowledge and approval.

This book will help you manage your allergy. It gives you the tools to make record keeping simple and convenient. And it should help you better understand a complex and perplexing disorder.

PERSONAL DATA

NAME ....

ADDRESS ....

....

....

TELEPHONE home .... work/school ....

IN CASE OF EMERGENCY NOTIFY ....

TELEPHONE home .... work/school ....

ADDRESS ....

....

....

PHYSICIAN'S NAME ....

TELEPHONE ....

ADDRESS ....

....

....

AMBULANCE AND/OR LOCAL EMERGENCY

NUMBER ....

LOCAL HOSPITAL ....

TELEPHONE ....

PERSONAL DATA

ADDRESS ....

....

....

HEALTH INSURANCE COMPANY ....

POLICY NUMBER ....

MAJOR MEDICAL INSURANCE COMPANY ....

POLICY NUMBER ....

MEDICAL HISTORY

DIAGNOSIS ....

....

....

....

....

....

....

....

....

....

....

....

MEDICATIONS

(Clip or staple a copy of your prescription(s) to the opposite side of this page)

DRUG ....

DOSAGE ....

DIRCTIONS FOR USE ....

POSSIBLE SIDE EFFECTS ....

....

DRUG ....

DOSAGE ....

DIRECTIONS FOR USE ....

....

POSSIBLE SIDE EFFECTS ....

....

DRUG ....

DOSAGE ....

DIRECTIONS FOR USE ....

....

POSSIBLE SIDE EFFECTS ....

....

OTHER DRUGS

DRUG ....

FOR THE FOLLOWING CONDITION ....

....

DOSAGE ....

DIRECTIONS FOR USE ....

....

POSSIBLE SIDE EFFECTS ....

....

....

DRUG ....

FOR THE FOLLOWING CONDITION ....

....

DOSAGE ....

DIRECTIONS FOR USE ....

....

POSSIBLE SIDE EFFECTS ....

....

....

PERSONAL DATA

DRUG ....

FOR THE FOLLOWING CONDITION ....

....

DOSAGE ....

DIRECTIONS FOR USE ....

....

POSSIBLE SIDE EFFECTS ....

....

....

DRUG ....

FOR THE FOLLOWING CONDITION ....

....

DOSAGE ....

DIRECTIONS FOR USE ....

....

POSSIBLE SIDE EFFECTS ....

....

....

....

DIARIES

▼

The following pages are designed to help you control your allergy or asthma. The first few can be used to record any symptoms you experience and the circumstances under which they occur. Describe your symptom(s) as fully as possible and note the circumstances under which it (they) occurred. What was the weather like? Where were you, indoors or out? Were you exercising? Had you eaten? When had you last taken an antihistamine or bronchodilator? Could your symptom be a side effect of medication you are taking or the result of combining more than one drug? What about alcohol? Describe how you responded.

There are also pages for use as a food diary if you are trying to determine whether any of your symptoms are due to food allergies. If so, you should make copies of the pages provided since you will have to keep track of your food intake for at least two weeks.

Following the food-diary pages, there are some additional pages for use as an exercise diary should your symptoms be associated with exercise, as they may be if you have asthma. Here, too, it is a good idea to make extra copies so you will have some blank diary pages should symptoms recur.

DIARY

DATE ....
SYMPTOM ....
DURATION ....
DESCRIPTION ....
....
CIRCUMSTANCES ....
....
RESPONSE ....
....

DATE ....
SYMPTOM ....
DURATION ....
DESCRIPTION ....
....
CIRCUMSTANCES ....
....
RESPONSE ....
....

DIARY

DATE ....

SYMPTOM ....

DURATION ....

DESCRIPTION ....

....

CIRCUMSTANCES ....

....

RESPONSE ....

....

DATE ....

SYMPTOM ....

DURATION ....

DESCRIPTION ....

....

CIRCUMSTANCES ....

....

RESPONSE ....

....

D IARY

DATE ....

SYMPTOM ....

DURATION ....

DESCRIPTION ....

....

CIRCUMSTANCES ....

....

RESPONSE ....

....

DATE ....

SYMPTOM ....

DURATION ....

DESCRIPTION ....

....

CIRCUMSTANCES ....

....

RESPONSE ....

....

DIARY

DATE ....

SYMPTOM ....

DURATION ....

DESCRIPTION ....

....

CIRCUMSTANCES ....

....

RESPONSE ....

....

DATE ....

SYMPTOM ....

DURATION ....

DESCRIPTION ....

....

CIRCUMSTANCES ....

....

RESPONSE ....

....

DIARY

DATE ....

SYMPTOM ....

DURATION ....

DESCRIPTION ....

....

CIRCUMSTANCES ....

....

RESPONSE ....

....

DATE ....

SYMPTOM ....

DURATION ....

DESCRIPTION ....

....

CIRCUMSTANCES ....

....

RESPONSE ....

....

DIARY

DATE ....

SYMPTOM ....

DURATION ....

DESCRIPTION ....

....

CIRCUMSTANCES ....

....

RESPONSE ....

....

DATE ....

SYMPTOM ....

DURATION ....

DESCRIPTION ....

....

CIRCUMSTANCES ....

....

RESPONSE ....

....

FOOD DIARY
(Sample Entry)

DATE: 5/3

<u>MEAL</u>

BREAKFAST (Time: 8 A.M.) Orange juice; Cereal with milk; Coffee with milk, sugar

LUNCH (Time: I P.M.) Tuna salad sandwich; Sour pickle; Potato chips; Iced tea

DINNER (Time: 6:30 P.M.) Tomato soup; Bread sticks; Tossed green salad, roquefort dressing; Broiled scallops; Baked potato with sour cream; Asparagus with lemon butter; Strawberry ice cream, 2 chocolate chip cookies; Tea with lemon, sugar

SNACKS (Time: late afternoon) Package roasted peanuts

SYMPTOMS Itching, hives beginning early evening.

FOOD DIARY

DATE:

<u>**MEAL**</u>

BREAKFAST (Time: _____)

....
....

LUNCH (Time: _____) ....

....
....

DINNER (Time: _____) ....

....
....
....

SNACKS (Times: _____)

....
....

SYMPTOMS: ....

....

F OOD DIARY

DATE:

<u>MEAL</u>

B R E A K F A S T (Time: _____)

....

....

L U N C H (Time: _____) ....

....

....

D I N N E R (Time: _____) ....

....

....

....

S N A C K S (Times: _____)

....

....

S Y M P T O M S : ....

....

FOOD DIARY

DATE:

<u>MEAL</u>

BREAKFAST (Time: _____)

....

....

LUNCH (Time: _____) ....

....

....

DINNER (Time: _____) ....

....

....

....

SNACKS (Times: _____)

....

....

SYMPTOMS: ....

....

F OOD DIARY

DATE:

<u>MEAL</u>

BREAKFAST (Time: _____)

....

....

LUNCH (Time: _____) ....

....

....

DINNER (Time: _____) ....

....

....

....

SNACKS (Times: _____)

....

....

SYMPTOMS: ....

....

FOOD DIARY

DATE:

<u>MEAL</u>

BREAKFAST (Time: _____)

....

....

LUNCH (Time: _____) ....

....

....

DINNER (Time: _____) ....

....

....

....

SNACKS (Times: _____)

....

....

SYMPTOMS: ....

....

F OOD DIARY

DATE:

<u>MEAL</u>

B R E A K F A S T (Time: _____)

....

....

L U N C H (Time: _____) ....

....

....

D I N N E R (Time: _____) ....

....

....

....

S N A C K S (Times: _____)

....

....

S Y M P T O M S: ....

....

EXERCISE DIARY
(Sample Entry)

DATE 9/15 ....

ACTIVITY Low impact aerobics ....

DURATION Approximately 25 minutes ....

SYMPTOM Tightness in chest, slight wheezing ....

DURATION Seven or eight minutes ....

RESPONSE Sat quietly, deep breathing, drank water ....

EXERCISE DIARY

DATE ....

ACTIVITY ....

DURATION ....

SYMPTOM ....

DURATION ....

RESPONSE ....

DATE ....

ACTIVITY ....

DURATION ....

SYMPTOM ....

DURATION ....

RESPONSE ....

DATE ....

ACTIVITY ....

DURATION ....

SYMPTOM ....

DURATION ....

RESPONSE ....

EXERCISE DIARY

DATE ....

ACTIVITY ....

DURATION ....

SYMPTOM ....

DURATION ....

RESPONSE ....

DATE ....

ACTIVITY ....

DURATION ....

SYMPTOM ....

DURATION ....

RESPONSE ....

DATE ....

ACTIVITY ....

DURATION ....

SYMPTOM ....

DURATION ....

RESPONSE ....

EXERCISE DIARY

DATE ....
ACTIVITY ....
DURATION ....
SYMPTOM ....
DURATION ....
RESPONSE ....

DATE ....
ACTIVITY ....
DURATION ....
SYMPTOM ....
DURATION ....
RESPONSE ....

DATE ....
ACTIVITY ....
DURATION ....
SYMPTOM ....
DURATION ....
RESPONSE ....

EXERCISE DIARY

DATE ....

ACTIVITY ....

DURATION ....

SYMPTOM ....

DURATION ....

RESPONSE ....

DATE ....

ACTIVITY ....

DURATION ....

SYMPTOM ....

DURATION ....

RESPONSE ....

DATE ....

ACTIVITY ....

DURATION ....

SYMPTOM ....

DURATION ....

RESPONSE ....

EXERCISE DIARY

DATE ....

ACTIVITY ....

DURATION ....

SYMPTOM ....

DURATION ....

RESPONSE ....

DATE ....

ACTIVITY ....

DURATION ....

SYMPTOM ....

DURATION ....

RESPONSE ....

DATE ....

ACTIVITY ....

DURATION ....

SYMPTOM ....

DURATION ....

RESPONSE ....

EXERCISE DIARY

DATE ....

ACTIVITY ....

DURATION ....

SYMPTOM ....

DURATION ....

RESPONSE ....

DATE ....

ACTIVITY ....

DURATION ....

SYMPTOM ....

DURATION ....

RESPONSE ....

DATE ....

ACTIVITY ....

DURATION ....

SYMPTOM ....

DURATION ....

RESPONSE ....

EMERGENCIES
▼

Place a paper clip or other marker on this page so you can turn to it quickly in the event of an emergency.

If you are the patient, you may need help to cope with an emergency. Ask your spouse, parent or other close relative, traveling companion, teacher or coach to read and become familiar with the instructions below.

Individuals with severe allergies or asthma should wear a Medic-Alert tag or bracelet so that emergency medical personnel will know how to proceed should you need help. To order Medic-Alert identification, telephone 1 (800) ID-ALERT. You should also carry a card in your wallet noting that you are allergic or asthmatic.

ANAPHYLAXIS

This is a life-threatening emergency that can affect people who are allergic to insect stings or certain foods or drugs. Anyone susceptible to these attacks should carry an emergency kit containing injectable epinephrine to bring symptoms under control.

Symptoms include:
- A red, itchy rash
- Hives
- Flushed face
- A feeling of apprehension
- Palpitations
- Fainting
- Feeling uncomfortably hot
- Dizziness
- Nausea, vomiting, diarrhea, abdominal cramps
- Shortness of breath
- Tightness in the chest
- Wheezing
- Loss of consciousness

Anaphylaxis requires immediate emergency action. There are two courses of action:
- Administer injectable epinephrine.
- Get immediate medical attention.

If no injectable epinephrine is available, telephone 911 or your local emergency number (please fill in the correct number): ....

Or rush the patient to the emergency room (please fill in the name and address of the nearest hospital):

....

....

....

Or call the patient's doctor and tell the nurse or service there is an emergency (please fill in the name, address and telephone number of the physician who treats your allergy):

If epinephrine is available, you must inject it immediately. There are two types of injectable epinephrine on the market, EpiPen and the AnaKit.

EpiPen is an automatic injector. Directions for use:

- Pull off the gray safety cap.
- Place the black tip on the outer thigh.
- Push the EpiPen against the skin and hold in place for several seconds. It will automatically inject a premeasured dose of epinephrine.

AnaKit provides a syringe with a preloaded, measured dose of epinephrine. Directions for use:

- Remove the protective sheath from the syringe.
- Inject the epinephrine into the outer thigh or upper arm.

After administering epinephrine, call the doctor listed above or take the patient to the hospital. Do this even if the patient protests. Further treatment may be needed to prevent a recurrence.

Additional Precautions

- Get a new supply of epinephrine after using the one you have.

- Periodically check the expiration date on your epinephrine emergency kit to be sure it will be effective should you need it.

ASTHMA

The following symptoms of a severe asthma attack demand emergency medical attention:
- Flared nostrils
- Holding the hands over the head
- Blue lips and/or fingernails
- Perspiration
- Raised shoulders
- Breathing from the neck up
- None of the self-treatment methods described in Chapter III are helping.

At this point, you need medical help:
- Call the doctor (fill in the name and telephone number of the physician who treats you—or your child —for asthma in the space provided below):

    Physician: ....

    Telephone: ....

- If the doctor is not available, take the patient to the hospital (fill in the name and address below):

    ....
    ....
    ....

- *Or* telephone 911 or your local emergency number (fill in the correct number):

....

- If the patient is a child and the attack takes place at school or elsewhere away from home, the parents or guardian should be notified as soon as possible after treatment has begun (please fill in the names and home and/or work telephone numbers of one or both parents or other responsible adult in the spaces provided below):

Name: ....

Relationship to child: ....

Telephone: Home ....

　　　　　　　Work ....

Name: ....

Relationship to child: ....

Telephone: Home ....

　　　　　　　Work ....

TRAVEL
CHECKLIST

▼

Here's what you'll need for vacations and/or business trips:

- Your Medic-Alert identification
- This book
- Copies of all your prescriptions (attach to page xxi)
- Enough medication and/or epinephrine. Pack them in a readily accessible bag you can keep with you. If you are traveling by airplane, do not check this bag with the rest of your luggage.
- A backup supply of epinephrine in another bag for use if your carry-on bag is lost or stolen. It is easier to take extras than it is to fill prescriptions and replace equipment, particularly if you are traveling abroad.
- If applicable, a doctor's note explaining that you have a severe allergy and must carry injectable epinephrine. When traveling abroad, this can help

avert awkwardness if security or customs officials question the syringe in your emergency kit.
- Make sure your traveling companions know you are susceptible to a severe allergic reaction. Ask them to read the section on emergencies beginning on page xlvii.

ALLERGIES

▼

A RANDOM HOUSE
PERSONAL
MEDICAL
HANDBOOK

OVERVIEW

▼

W E tend to use the term *allergy* rather loosely, invoking it to explain everything from personal likes and dislikes to genuine physical reactions to foods, pollen and insect stings. A new, unproved theory of allergy holds that foods, chemicals and/or environmental pollutants are also responsible for a wide range of common but vague symptoms ranging from headaches to behavior problems in children. Strictly speaking, allergy has a very specific meaning: an abnormal immune-system reaction to ordinarily harmless substances. Symptoms can be merely uncomfortable (the sneezing and runny nose of hay fever), alarming and dangerous (asthmatic wheezing) and even life-threatening (anaphylactic shock, a frighteningly rapid reaction that requires emergency treatment).

No one knows for sure exactly how many people suffer from allergies. A conservative estimate from the National Institute of Allergy and Infectious Diseases holds that one out of every six Americans has some sort of allergy. The vast majority, more than 22 million, suffer from hay fever; nearly 10 million more have asthma, and almost 12 million are allergic to certain foods, drugs or insect stings, or have skin problems like eczema and hives caused by allergies. Included in this total are 6 million children with hay fever or similar allergies, 2 to 3 million with asthma and 2 million with allergic eczema. Each of these conditions will be discussed separately in subsequent chapters.

THE IMMUNE SYSTEM

The key to an understanding of allergy is the immune system, the body's defense mechanism against viruses, bacteria, parasites and other threats to health. Enormously complex, our immune system can distinguish between the cells, tissues, etc., that belong in our bodies and invading microorganisms that could cause disease. Normally, it also can tell the difference between harmless substances and dangerous ones.

Because it is capable of "remembering" a previous attacker—say, the virus that causes a cold—it will forever protect you from another attack by that particular germ. Since hundreds of viruses are capable of causing colds, you won't be immune from colds in general. But never again will your sniffles be due to any of the viruses that caused your previous colds. This is why, as we get older, we tend to get fewer and fewer colds. Similarly, once we've had certain childhood illnesses—measles and mumps, for instance—we'll never get them again.

When it malfunctions, the immune system can be very dangerous indeed, sometimes attacking the body's own tissues as if they were threats to health. A number of diseases, including rheumatoid arthritis and systemic lupus erythematosis, stem from faulty immune responses. Allergies are due to an immune system peculiarity, an overabundance of a disease-fighting substance or antibody called immunoglobulin E (IgE).

Antigens and Allergens

Any substance that triggers the immune system to spring into action is called an antigen. In response to the arrival of an antigen, certain white blood cells (B cells), produce antibodies also known as immunoglobulins. There are several different types of immunoglobulins, each with a different role in preserving health:

- IgA, found in saliva and tears, is our first line of defense against microorganisms entering the body via the respiratory and digestive tracts.
- IgD is mysterious; we know it exists but don't understand what role it plays in immunity.
- IgE, the antibody responsible for allergic reactions, ordinarily leads the immune-system defense against parasitic worms.
- IgG activates so-called "scavenger" cells that scoop up and destroy antigens; it also has other complex tasks not relevant here.
- IgM plays the largest role in immune reactions to harmful antigens.

When an antigen enters the body, antibodies or immunoglobulins attach to them, setting them up for destruction by other elements of the immune system. You have antibodies for every antigen that has ever entered your body. And as long as your immune system remains healthy, it will continue to produce antibodies to any new antigen.

IMMUNOGLOBULIN E (IgE)

Normally, we have only small amounts of IgE. Because this type of antibody was intended to fend off parasitic worms, people from tropical areas of the world where parasitic diseases are most common have higher levels than those from more temperate regions. However, people with allergies have abnormally high levels of IgE.

When allergy is present and an ordinarily harmless substance like ragweed pollen enters the body, it is perceived as an antigen. IgE then binds the pollen to cells called *mast cells* and *basophils*. These cells contain mediators, chemicals that enable them to fight disease. Among them is *histamine,* considered responsible for sneezing, itching and other symptoms typical of allergy.

A number of other mediators play a role in allergy:
- Leukotrines, which may be more potent than histamine in the bronchial constriction of allergic asthma
- Eosinophil Chemotactic Factor of Anaphylaxis (ECF-A), which attracts blood cells to the area of the body where an allergic reaction is taking place
- Prostaglandins, fatty acids whose role in allergy is unclear
- Bradykinin, an enzyme that can dilate (widen) blood vessels

- Serotonin, an enzyme that can stimulate secretion of mucus and cause smooth muscle to contract

HEREDITY

Because the tendency to overproduce IgE is inherited, allergies run in families. If one parent is allergic, each child has a chance of developing an allergy; if both parents are allergic, two out of three of their children are likely to be allergic, too. However, specific allergies are not necessarily passed from one generation to the next. The child of someone with hay fever won't necessarily develop an allergy to ragweed pollen.

Nevertheless, in some instances the gene for a specific allergy may be inherited, although whether the allergy itself actually develops depends on exposure. For instance, if you inherit a tendency toward hay fever and live in a ragweed-free area, you may never know you have hay fever. It is also believed that some people inherit high levels of IgE but never develop allergies because of a genetic glitch that prevents mast cells and basophils from releasing histamine and other symptom-producing substances in response to the allergen.

ALLERGY SYMPTOMS

In general, allergy symptoms develop along the route the allergen follows as it enters the body. Thus, allergies to inhaled substances like dust and pollen usually involve the respiratory tract. Typical symptoms include sneezing, runny nose, wheezing and chest tightness characteristic of asthma. Food-allergy symptoms usually affect the digestive tract but may include hives, wheezing, eczema or anaphylaxis. Skin symptoms like hives, rashes and itching are typical of contact dermatitis, allergy to substances that touch the body.

The most dangerous symptom of all is anaphylaxis, a sudden, rapidly progressing and potentially fatal allergic reaction. Symptoms usually begin almost immediately after exposure to the allergen. They include redness, swelling and sometimes hives. As the reaction progresses, vomiting, abdominal cramps and diarrhea may develop. If swelling affects the larynx or causes bronchial spasm, breathing can become difficult. A drop in blood pressure can send the victim into shock. Anaphylaxis requires immediate emergency treatment. (See the Emergencies section on page xlvii for instructions.)

The following allergens can trigger anaphylaxis in susceptible people:
- Drugs, particularly penicillin and other antibiotics
- Insect stings
- Foods, principally peanuts, eggs, wheat, milk, shellfish and tree nuts
- Contrast dyes used for X rays of the kidneys, gallbladder, arteries to the heart and brain

Although anaphylaxis usually develops only after an initial exposure to a substance that sets the stage for the cascade of allergic events, it can occur for reasons that never become clear and recur repeatedly for no apparent reason. In these *idiopathic* (cause unknown) cases, victims haven't come in contact with any of the drugs, foods or insects usually associated with anaphylaxis.

Anyone who has had one anaphylactic reaction is in danger of having another on subsequent exposure to the allergen responsible. For this reason, victims must always be vigilant about avoiding the allergen (given that they know what it is) and protect themselves by having at hand an emergency kit containing injectable epinephrine.

No one knows how many people are subject to anaphylactic reactions or why some people with allergies develop them, but thankfully most do not. However, an allergy to anything (pollen, dust, etc.) increases the risk that you will have an anaphylactic reaction to drugs, foods or insect stings, the triggers that often cause anaphylactic episodes.

ALLERGY TREATMENT

Doctors who specialize in allergy treatment practice a type of medicine known as *clinical immunology*. However, dermatologists, physicians who specialize in treating skin disorders, can treat allergy symptoms involving the skin, and gastroenterologists sometimes treat food allergies. Depending on your symptoms and the severity of your allergy, your family physician may refer you to a specialist in allergy or dermatology. To find a specialist on your own, look for a doctor who has had advanced training in allergy and immunology. You can verify a doctor's credentials and training in the *Direc-*

tory of Medical Specialists, available in most public libraries. Your local medical society may be able to refer you to specialists in allergy and/or dermatology in your area, and you can also find a specialist by telephoning the appropriate department at the nearest large hospital.

CLINICAL ECOLOGY

Clinical ecology, sometimes called environmental medicine, is a controversial medical specialty practiced by physicians who believe that a wide range of physical, and sometimes emotional, disorders are due to allergies to food, low levels of environmental pollutants in the air and/or chemicals used in the manufacture of synthetic fabrics and other man-made materials.

Among the symptoms attributed to allergies or sensitivities to these chemicals are fatigue, depression, headache, dizziness, irritability, anxiety, mood swings, memory lapses, confusion, nausea, palpitations, constipation, and muscle and joint aches. All are common symptoms that can stem from any number of physical or emotional conditions, including depression, an emotional disorder that affects an estimated 8 million Americans per year. Indeed, independent evaluations of some of the patients diagnosed as having environmental allergies indicate that their symptoms were due to depression, or an anxiety disorder, or another form of psychiatric illness.

Certain tests and treatments recommended by these practitioners have not been scientifically validated. See

Chapter VII for a discussion of both conventional and unconventional allergy testing, and Chapter VIII for a description of proven and unproven allergy-treatment methods.

HAY FEVER

▼

E VERYONE knows what hay fever is even though the allergy in question has nothing to do with either hay or fever. The term itself is a holdover from the notion that hay pitching at summer's end was responsible for the sneezing and sniffling that afflicts so many people at that time of year. The real culprit, of course, is pollen from weeds. The "fever" in hay fever probably is an artifact from the days when any ailment was described as a fever.

The correct medical name for hay fever is *seasonal allergic rhinitis,* meaning inflammation of the nose due to an allergy that recurs from season to season. The allergens responsible are pollen from weeds, grasses and trees. The one most often to blame is ragweed pollen dispersed during the late summer in most of the United States except for the West Coast, the northern tip of Maine and the southern tip of Florida. Ragweed plays no part in allergic rhinitis that occurs during the spring and early summer when grass and tree pollen are circulating. Allergies to these pollens sometimes are mistakenly described as "rose fever" since they occur when roses come into bloom. People allergic to grass and/or tree pollen *and* ragweed or other weed pollen may not get a break from their symptoms from early spring until after the hay-fever season in the fall.

Similar symptoms that occur throughout the year may be due to allergies to dust, animal dander and molds, and are known medically as *perennial allergic rhinitis*. Whatever the cause, the symptoms are the same, although severity varies from person to person and, with seasonal allergies like hay fever, from year to year. Among them:

- Sneezing and, often, a runny or stuffy nose
- Itching eyes, nose and throat
- Dark circles under the eyes sometimes called "allergic shiners," due to restricted blood flow around the sinuses
- Watering eyes
- Conjunctivitis (inflammation of the membrane lining the eyelids; eyes may itch and the lids are red-rimmed)

Contending with these symptoms can be tiring and emotionally draining. You may lack energy, have little or no appetite, become irritable and sometimes depressed.

Symptoms of allergic rhinitis are set off when pollen is inhaled and interacts with IgE on sensitized mast cells (see Chapter I). These cells then release histamine and other chemical mediators that dilate small blood vessels in the nose. Fluid seeps out of the affected vessels and swells the nasal passages, causing congestion and setting in motion the other symptoms. Although colds, flu and allergies are the best-known causes of sneezing and other nasal symptoms, in many cases other conditions are to blame:

- Vasomotor rhinitis, a *nonallergic* disorder of unknown cause, is believed responsible for *between 60 and 70 percent* of all cases of chronic rhinitis.
- *Nasal polyps* that form in the sinuses can bulge out into the nose, clog nasal passages and interfere with the sense of smell. These polyps are not tumors and, apart from the discomfort they cause, are not dangerous. However, they may have to be removed surgically to permanently relieve symptoms.
- The septum, the bone that divides the nose, can obstruct nasal passages on either side of the nose if it deviates from its normal configuration. You can be born with a *deviated septum,* or an injury may alter normal septum structure. If symptoms cannot be tolerated, a deviated septum can be corrected surgically.
- *Eosinophilic, nonallergenic rhinitis,* a disorder that can appear suddenly for no apparent reason, can cause nasal symptoms. Eosinophils, the blood cells usually found with allergy, are present in nasal secretions. It is treated with the same drugs used to control hay fever.
- *Neutrophilic rhinosinusitis* usually stems from a sinus infection but may begin with a cold or flu. It is treated with antibiotics and drugs also used to control hay fever.
- *Primary vasomotor instability,* a condition that may develop during pregnancy, causes nasal con-

gestion that can be treated with decongestants and other drugs.

- *Rhinitis medicamentosa,* a condition induced by overuse of nonprescription nasal-decongestant sprays and drops, often disappears when you stop using the decongestants, although it may take treatment with steroid nasal sprays to relieve symptoms and restore nasal passages to normal.

POLLEN

Pollen, the male reproductive cells of plants and trees, are microscopic in size, even tinier in diameter than a human hair. Some, such as ragweed pollen, are highly allergenic. Others aren't particularly important in causing allergy. For instance, florists and gardeners are usually the only people with allergies to the sticky flowering-plant pollen.

Pollen capable of triggering most allergic reactions usually is carried from plant to plant by the wind. If this doesn't seem like a very efficient method of fertilization, consider that a single ragweed plant can produce up to a million grains of pollen *per day* and that the pollen itself is so light and dry that it can ride the wind for many, many miles. Ragweed pollen has been found two miles high in the air and four hundred miles out to sea! Other plants that produce pollen associated with allergies include sagebrush, redroot pigweed, lamb's quarters, Russian thistle (tumbleweed) and English plantain.

Hay fever that develops in the early spring usually is

due to allergies to grass or tree pollen. Timothy, Bermuda, orchard, sweet vernal, red top and some blue grasses all produce allergenic pollen. So do the following trees: elm, birch, ash, hickory, poplar, sycamore, maple, cypress and walnut.

Allergic rhinitis usually develops before age forty, but new cases can occur at any age. It may disappear completely after a few seasons, but untreated cases usually worsen year by year until symptoms finally level off. Some patients with this condition also have or develop asthma. Another potential complication, sinusitis, is discussed later in this chapter.

Timing

The onset of seasonal allergies to pollen depends on where you live and the particular type of pollen responsible for your allergy. The charts on pages 17 to 20 present state-by-state information on when tree, grass and ragweed or other weed allergies occur. The weather can advance or delay the allergy season to some degree, and daily pollen counts will vary depending on the weather. Pollen levels generally are highest on warm, dry, breezy days and lowest when it is raining, chilly or damp. However, even pollen counts as low as twenty grains per cubic meter can cause symptoms in some patients.

Diagnosis and Treatment

Symptoms that appear and disappear on a seasonal basis strongly suggest a pollen allergy. However, you

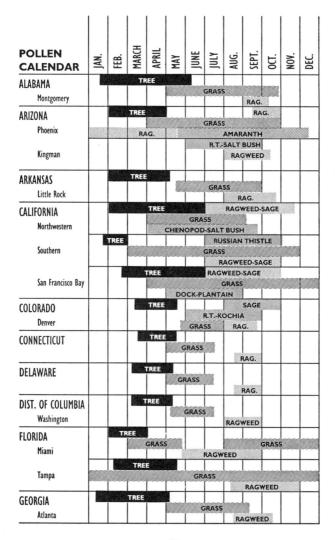

POLLEN CALENDAR

POLLEN CALENDAR	JAN.	FEB.	MARCH	APRIL	MAY	JUNE	JULY	AUG.	SEPT.	OCT.	NOV.	DEC.
ALABAMA Montgomery		TREE				GRASS				RAG.		
ARIZONA Phoenix		TREE			GRASS				RAG.			
		RAG.				AMARANTH						
Kingman					R.T.-SALT BUSH			RAGWEED				
ARKANSAS Little Rock		TREE				GRASS			RAG.			
CALIFORNIA Northwestern			TREE			RAGWEED-SAGE						
			GRASS									
			CHENOPOD-SALT BUSH									
Southern		TREE				RUSSIAN THISTLE						
			GRASS									
			RAGWEED-SAGE									
San Francisco Bay			TREE		RAGWEED-SAGE							
				GRASS								
			DOCK-PLANTAIN									
COLORADO Denver			TREE			SAGE						
			R.T.-KOCHIA									
			GRASS		RAG.							
CONNECTICUT			TREE		GRASS				RAG.			
DELAWARE			TREE		GRASS				RAG.			
DIST. OF COLUMBIA Washington			TREE		GRASS			RAGWEED				
FLORIDA Miami		TREE		GRASS			GRASS					
				RAGWEED								
Tampa		TREE			GRASS				RAGWEED			
GEORGIA Atlanta		TREE			GRASS			RAGWEED				

17

POLLEN CALENDAR (Continued)

STATE / City	JAN.	FEB.	MARCH	APRIL	MAY	JUNE	JULY	AUG.	SEPT.	OCT.	NOV.	DEC.
IDAHO Southern			TREE	TREE	GRASS	GRASS	R.T.-SALT BUSH	SAGE / RAG.	SAGE			
ILLINOIS Chicago			TREE	TREE	GRASS	GRASS		RAG.	RAG.			
INDIANA Indianapolis			TREE	TREE	GRASS	GRASS		RAG.	RAG.			
IOWA Ames				TREE		GRASS	GRASS	RAG.				
KANSAS Wichita				TREE	GRASS	GRASS	R. T.-AMAR.	RAGWEED	RAGWEED			
KENTUCKY Louisville			TREE	TREE	GRASS	GRASS		RAGWEED	RAGWEED			
LOUISIANA New Orleans	TREE	TREE			GRASS	GRASS	GRASS	GRASS / RAGWEED	GRASS / RAGWEED			
MAINE				TREE	GRASS	GRASS		RAG.				
MARYLAND Baltimore			TREE	TREE	GRASS	GRASS		RAGWEED	RAGWEED			
MASSACHUSETTS Boston				TREE	GRASS	GRASS		RAG.				
MICHIGAN Detroit			TREE	TREE	GRASS	GRASS		RAG.				
MINNESOTA Minneapolis				TREE	GRASS	CHEN-AMAR / GRASS	CHEN-AMAR	RAG.				
MISSISSIPPI Vicksburg		TREE	TREE		GRASS	GRASS	GRASS	GRASS	GRASS / RAG.			
MISSOURI St. Louis			TREE	TREE	GRASS	CHEN-AMAR / GRASS	CHEN-AMAR	RAGWEED	RAGWEED			
Kansas City			TREE	TREE	GRASS	CHEN-AMAR / GRASS	CHEN-AMAR	RAGWEED	RAGWEED			

18

	JAN.	FEB.	MARCH	APRIL	MAY	JUNE	JULY	AUG.	SEPT.	OCT.	NOV.	DEC.
MONTANA Miles City				TREE				RAG.-SAGE				
					GRASS							
						R. THISTLE						
NEBRASKA Omaha			TREE				R. THISTLE					
					GRASS		HEMP					
								RAG.				
NEVADA Reno				TREE				RAG.				
					GRASS		SAGE					
					R.T.-SALT BUSH							
NEW HAMPSHIRE				TREE								
					GRASS							
							RAG.					
NEW JERSEY				TREE								
					GRASS							
							RAGWEED					
NEW MEXICO Roswell		TREE						RAG-SAGE				
						GRASS						
					AMAR.-SALT BUSH							
NEW YORK New York City				TREE								
					GRASS							
							RAGWEED					
NORTH CAROLINA Raleigh		TREE					GRASS					
								RAGWEED				
NORTH DAKOTA Fargo				TREE			RUSS. THISTLE					
					GRASS		SAGE					
						RAGWEED						
OHIO Cleveland				TREE								
					GRASS							
							RAGWEED					
OKLAHOMA Oklahoma City			TREE				AMARANTH					
					GRASS							
								RAGWEED				
OREGON Portland			TREE									
					GRASS							
					DOCK-PLANTAIN							
East of Cascade Mountains			TREE			GRASS	SAGE					
					R.T.-SALT BUSH							
							RAG.					
PENNSYLVANIA				TREE								
					GRASS							
							RAG.					

19

POLLEN CALENDAR (Continued)

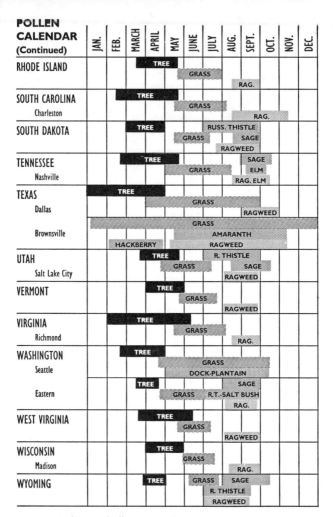

	JAN.	FEB.	MARCH	APRIL	MAY	JUNE	JULY	AUG.	SEPT.	OCT.	NOV.	DEC.
RHODE ISLAND			TREE	TREE	GRASS	GRASS	GRASS	RAG.	RAG.			
SOUTH CAROLINA Charleston		TREE	TREE	TREE	GRASS	GRASS	GRASS		RAG.	RAG.		
SOUTH DAKOTA			TREE	TREE		GRASS	GRASS / RUSS. THISTLE / RAGWEED	RUSS. THISTLE / RAGWEED	SAGE			
TENNESSEE Nashville		TREE	TREE	TREE		GRASS	GRASS	SAGE / RAG. ELM	SAGE / ELM			
TEXAS Dallas	TREE	TREE	TREE	GRASS	GRASS	GRASS	GRASS	GRASS / RAGWEED	GRASS / RAGWEED	RAGWEED		
Brownsville	GRASS / HACKBERRY	GRASS / HACKBERRY	GRASS / HACKBERRY	GRASS / HACKBERRY	GRASS	GRASS	GRASS / RAGWEED	GRASS / AMARANTH / RAGWEED	GRASS / AMARANTH / RAGWEED	GRASS / AMARANTH / RAGWEED	GRASS	GRASS
UTAH Salt Lake City				TREE	TREE / GRASS	GRASS / R. THISTLE	R. THISTLE / RAGWEED	SAGE / RAGWEED	SAGE			
VERMONT				TREE	TREE / GRASS	GRASS		RAGWEED	RAGWEED			
VIRGINIA Richmond			TREE	TREE	GRASS	GRASS		RAG.	RAG.			
WASHINGTON Seattle			TREE	GRASS	GRASS / DOCK-PLANTAIN	GRASS / DOCK-PLANTAIN	GRASS / DOCK-PLANTAIN	GRASS / DOCK-PLANTAIN	GRASS / DOCK-PLANTAIN			
Eastern			TREE	TREE	GRASS	GRASS	R.T.-SALT BUSH	SAGE / R.T.-SALT BUSH / RAG.	SAGE / RAG.			
WEST VIRGINIA			TREE	TREE	GRASS	GRASS		RAGWEED	RAGWEED			
WISCONSIN Madison				TREE	GRASS	GRASS		RAG.	RAG.			
WYOMING				TREE		GRASS	GRASS / SAGE / R. THISTLE / RAGWEED	SAGE / R. THISTLE / RAGWEED				

SOURCE: *Asthma and Allergies: An Optimistic Future*, U.S. Department of Health and Human Services.

may need tests to determine exactly which pollen is to blame. Allergy testing is discussed in Chapter VII.

As with any allergy, the most effective treatment is avoiding the substance that triggers symptoms. When pollen is the problem, avoidance is almost impossible. You might be able to escape by moving to an area where the pollen-producing plant responsible for your particular allergy does not grow, but there is always the possibility that you will develop an allergy to another type of pollen in your new locale. However, you may be able to escape the worst of the pollen season by scheduling your vacation to coincide.

If you can't get away, antihistamines available over the counter and nonprescription nasal decongestant drops or sprays can provide some relief. Be very careful with the decongestants. Overuse can lead to *rhinitis medicamentosa* (see page 102). These drugs cause a "rebound" effect, so that you require more to get relief; eventually, it doesn't help at all, and your nasal congestion becomes worse than it was when you first started using the drug. Treatment with prescription corticosteroids may be needed to reverse this condition.

Your doctor may prescribe stronger antihistamines, decongestants, nasal steroid inhalants, cromolyn or other drugs to relieve your hay-fever symptoms. (See Chapter IX.) If nothing else helps, your doctor may recommend immunotherapy, injections of diluted extracts of the pollen to which you are allergic. (See Chapter VIII.)

In addition to medical treatment, the following measures may help reduce or control hay-fever symptoms:

- Stay indoors in the early morning; pollen counts are highest between 5:00 A.M. and 10:00 A.M.
- Wear a face mask designed to filter pollen out of the air if you must work out of doors during hay-fever season.
- Use an air conditioner at home or in your car to filter out pollen.
- Avoid mowing lawns and freshly cut grass; pollen levels are high after mowing.
- Avoid raking leaves during the pollen season.
- Dry clothes and bed linen in automatic driers, not on an outdoor clothesline; pollen can collect in clothes and linen.
- Air-filtering devices made with fiberglass or electrically charged plates can be attached to home heating and cooling systems; portable filtering devices are also available to keep indoor air pollen-free. Ask your doctor to recommend which type of filter is best for your condition. The National Institute of Allergy and Infectious Diseases (NIAID) recommends that before buying, you rent a portable filter for a month or two to see if it helps. Make sure the device you are considering is big enough to exchange the air in the room five or six times per hour.
- Check the ozone output of the filter you are considering; ozone can worsen allergy symptoms by irritating the nose and airways. High efficiency particulate air filters (HEPA) do not release ozone into the air.
- Avoid dust, smoke, insect sprays, air pollution and

paint or tar fumes, all of which can worsen allergy symptoms.

DUST

There is a lot more to house dust than meets the eye. It is composed of fabrics, lint, feathers, bacteria, mold, fungus spores, food particles, human and animal hair and dander (skin) and dust mites, microscopically small insects that live on surfaces of mattresses and flooring and feed on tiny bits of human skin and animal dander that are constantly being shed. If you have a pet, there is a good chance that its dander is responsible for your allergy.

House dust is usually to blame for perennial allergic rhinitis. The symptoms of this type of allergy are identical to those caused by pollen except for the fact that their "season" never ends.

Dust Mites

Dust mites are now considered responsible for many, if not most, perennial allergic rhinitis as well as asthma (see Chapter III) and certain allergic skin conditions (see Chapter V). These tiny insects flourish in humid conditions. The mites in whole or in part are found everywhere dust accumulates, but the largest concentrations are in bedding, upholstery and carpeting. Vacuuming or other activities that raise dust may propel dust mites into the air.

Testing and Treatment

You can confirm that an allergy to dust is to blame for chronic allergic rhinitis with tests in which extracts of dust or dust mites are injected or applied to a skin scratch (see Chapter VII).

Allergy symptoms can be treated with the same drugs used to treat hay fever, and sometimes with allergy shots, to desensitize patients to the dust mites. Shots appear to work better in children than adults (see Chapter VIII). As with any allergy, the most effective treatment is avoidance.

Dust and Dust-Mite Control

No matter how clean your home, it is almost impossible to completely eliminate dust and dust mites. Still, the following measures often can help relieve symptoms by reducing dust and the dust-mite population:

- Avoid carpeting; if you do have carpets, vacuum thoroughly; however, this won't eliminate live mites or embedded remains of dead ones. If possible, cover floors with area rugs that can be washed frequently.
- Avoid upholstered furniture, which traps dust and provides a good environment for mites.
- Wash *all* bedding in hot water every seven to ten days.
- Enclose mattress in heavy vinyl plastic with zippered closure and cover the plastic with a washable mattress pad.

- Use a dehumidifier or air conditioner when the humidity is high.
- Damp mop floors daily and dust daily with a damp cloth.
- Clean bedrooms weekly; this includes walls, ceiling, closets and the backs and bottoms of furniture.
- Avoid feather or kapok pillows (use polyester fiberfill).
- If possible, have someone else do housecleaning; wear a disposable surgical face mask if you must clean.
- Avoid bunk beds and beds with canopies.
- Clean air-conditioning and heating filters every month.
- If possible, keep hot-air registers closed; clean air ducts periodically; place filters on hot-air registers and change them frequently.
- Use dust-removing polishes on floors, woodwork and furniture.
- Eliminate as many dust collectors as possible, including knicknacks, stuffed animals, unnecessary pillows, books and magazines.
- Avoid fuzzy or electric blankets.
- Don't spend time in basement living areas, which tend to be damp and hospitable to dust mites.
- Avoid irritating inhalants, including tobacco smoke, insect sprays, paint and tar fumes.

MOLDS

Microscopic spores from unseen molds that thrive on moisture are a frequent cause of allergic rhinitis that occurs seasonally or, in warm climates, all year round.

In the house, molds can be found in damp basements and closets, bathrooms, food-storage areas, the drip trays under refrigerators, in air conditioners, humidifiers, garbage pails, mattresses, upholstered furniture and old foam-rubber pillows. Outdoor molds grow in clumps of rotting leaves, in moist shady areas of gardens and compost piles.

Millions of spores can be wind-borne at any one time, but only a few molds produce spores light enough to cause allergies when inhaled. The most common are Alternaria and Cladosporium, found throughout the United States.

Allergies to molds are diagnosed and treated in the same way as hay fever and dust allergies. In addition, the following measures can reduce exposure to mold spores:

- Avoid damp basements and other areas listed above.
- Make sure leaves do not accumulate on the lawn or in the yard; if possible, do not remove them yourself. If you must collect leaves, wear a dust mask.
- Avoid driving in the country on dry, windy days when crops are being harvested.
- Dry out damp rooms or a damp basement with a dehumidifier, but beware: These machines are mold collectors and must be cleaned often.

- Use an air conditioner or air cleaner to reduce indoor mold levels; see the section on dust removal above for more on these devices.
- Keep small electric lights burning in closets to reduce humidity and discourage mold growth. *(Be careful: Too large a bulb in an enclosed space can be a fire hazard.)*
- Follow the cleaning recommendations listed in the section on dust removal, above.
- Keep dried plants and flowers out of the house; they provide an ideal environment for mold growth.
- Treat indoor areas that foster mold growth with special paints or chemicals; these include trioxy-methylene powder and crystals of paradichloroben-zene; silica gel, activated alumina or calcium chloride can discourage mold growth by absorbing moisture. These chemicals are not dangerous. Ask your pharmacist where to find them, and carefully follow directions for use. Most paint stores carry mold-inhibiting paints.

Hypersensitivity Pneumonitis

Inhaling certain molds on a regular basis can cause a number of disorders that fall under the general heading of allergic or hypersensitivity pneumonitis. Symptoms include cough, fever, chills and shortness of breath. These disorders usually affect people who are routinely exposed to molds that contaminate their work environment. The best-known example is farmer's lung, an illness due to inhaling spores from molds that grow on hay

CAUSES OF HYPERSENSITIVITY PNEUMONITIS

DISEASE	EXPOSURE
Farmer's lung	Moldy hay and other fodder
Bagassosis	Moldy sugar cane
Mushroom worker's disease	Mushroom compost
Humidifier lung	Contaminated system
Air conditioner lung	Contaminated system
Malt worker's disease	Moldy malt
Sauna taker's disease	Contaminated appliance
Bird fancier's disease	Pigeon, budgerigar, parrot, hen, turkey droppings
Maple bark stripper's disease	Mold maple logs
Sequoiosis	Moldy redwood sawdust
Wood pulp worker's disease	Moldy logs
Pituitary snuff taker's disease	Desiccated pituitary
Suberosis	Moldy cork dust
Cheesewasher's disease	Cheese mold
Wheat weevil disease	Wheat flour
Furrier's lung	Hair dust
Coffee worker's lung	Coffee dust
New Guinea lung	Thatched roof dust

SOURCE: *Asthma and Allergies: An Optimistic Future*, U.S. Department of Health and Human Services.

and other fodder. The chart on page 28 lists the various forms of hypersensitivity pneumonitis and their causes.

Since the symptoms of these disorders are so similar to those of the common cold or flu, diagnosis can be difficult. In most cases, the acute illness subsides in a few days, but less obvious forms of the disease can develop and lead to permanent lung damage. Anyone routinely exposed to any of the substances listed on the chart on page 28 who develops a chronic cough, shortness of breath, fatigue and unexplained weight loss could be suffering from subacute or chronic hypersensitivity pneumonitis. Avoiding the molds responsible and treatment with corticosteroids can often reverse the disorder or prevent it from worsening.

SINUSITIS

Allergies that affect the nose can cause sinusitis, inflammation of the sinuses, or hollow air spaces in the bone that surrounds the nose. Because the sinuses open into the nose, nasal obstruction due to allergies, colds, flu or other infections can trap air in the sinuses—or prevent air from reaching the sinuses—causing intense pain. A classic sinus headache is present when you wake up in the morning, but isn't necessarily restricted to the forehead.

The typical pain depends on which sinus is inflamed:
- The frontal sinuses located in the brow area over the eyes: pain in the forehead
- Maxillary sinuses inside each cheekbone: pain in the upper jaw and teeth; tenderness in the cheeks

- Ethmoid sinuses behind the bridge of the nose: pain around the eyes; swollen eyelids; tenderness on the sides of the nose, stuffy nose, loss of sense of smell
- Sphenoid sinuses above the ethmoids: earaches, neck pain, ache on top of the head. (These sinuses are less susceptible to inflammation than the others.)

Pain is not the only symptom of sinusitis. Postnasal drip occurs when mucus drains from the nose to the throat, sometimes causing irritation.

Managing Sinusitis

If you have allergic rhinitis of any type, it may not be possible to prevent sinusitis completely. Sinusitis is often due to a bacterial infection and requires treatment with an antibiotic. See your physician if you have sinusitis and are running a fever. In general, the better your allergy is controlled, the less trouble your sinuses will cause. The following are measures you can take to reduce the discomfort:

- Use a humidifier in dry rooms.
- Avoid alcohol; it causes membranes in the nose and sinuses to swell.
- Avoid chlorinated swimming pools; the chlorine irritates nasal and sinus membranes.
- Use decongestant nose drops or spray before traveling by airplane; changes in air pressure when you fly can cause discomfort.
- Inhale steam from a teakettle or vaporizer.
- Apply hot, wet compresses to the painful area.

- Use nasal decongestants occasionally and sparingly to open blocked nasal passages. Overuse can worsen symptoms. Saline nosedrops are safe and may help.

RHINITIS IN CHILDREN

An estimated 5 million children and adolescents in the United States suffer from hay fever and other forms of allergic rhinitis. Treatment is the same as it would be for adults except for appropriate adjustments in drug dosages. Often immunotherapy (allergy shots) is more helpful in children than in adults (see Chapter VIII).

Although some children may outgrow allergies, these disorders should never be ignored. They can result in a number of complications, including dental disorders (development of an "overbite" that may require orthodontia), sinus problems and an ear inflammation known as serous otitis media that can cause some degree of temporary and sometimes permanent hearing loss. Children with hay fever and other forms of allergic rhinitis are also susceptible to eczema, a skin condition (see Chapter V).

Serous Otitis Media

Although this middle-ear inflammation is a common disorder in children, it is particularly prevalent in those with allergic rhinitis. Caused by accumulation of fluid in the middle ear, the symptoms of serous otitis media may include pain, pressure or a "bubbling" sensation in the ear and a popping sound. Treatment with decongestants can reduce the inflammation; occasionally, the accumulated fluid may have to be aspirated, and in severe cases surgery may be needed to remove the adenoids if they are contributing to the problem. And, of course, the underlying allergy must be treated appropriately.

ASTHMA

▼

ASTHMA, a disorder of the lungs and bronchial tubes, has been known since ancient times but still defies precise medical definition. The problem is that the cause is not well understood and that asthma itself can differ dramatically from patient to patient. Some can be free of attack for years on end without treatment; others require lifelong attention, and still others have only sporadic attacks that subside when treated promptly. However it manifests itself, asthma is a chronic disease that can be controlled but not cured. It is not contagious or progressive. Except in severe cases, asthma doesn't damage the lungs or the network of bronchial tubes that carry air in and out of the body.

But the airways of asthma victims do respond abnormally to a wide variety of allergic and nonallergic substances. No one knows what underlies this so-called "hyperreactivity" (sometimes referred to as "twitchy" lungs). Heredity certainly plays some role. As with allergy itself, you are more likely to be asthmatic if one or both of your parents is affected. But researchers can only speculate about what differentiates hyperreactive from normal airways.

The onset of asthma is equally mysterious. Although allergy underlies most cases that develop in childhood and among adults under the age of forty, an upper respiratory infection—a cold, flu or bronchitis—usually precipitates the first attack; subsequent infections can cause asthma symptoms regardless of the allergic component of the disorder.

The allergens usually associated with asthma are dust and its constituents (dust mites, animal dander) and pollens (from weeds, grass and trees). Less often, allergies to certain foods, principally nuts, wheat, shellfish, eggs or milk, are to blame.

Many people with allergic or nonallergic asthma will develop attacks in response to aspirin. In rare cases, attacks may be triggered by tartrazine (the yellow food coloring in some cake mixes, candies, gelatins, commercially prepared desserts and citrus-fruit-flavored drinks) and sulfiting agents sometimes used to retard spoilage of fresh fruits, vegetables, fish and seafood and to enhance the appearance of certain processed foods. Strictly speaking, this intolerance is not an allergy because it isn't mediated by IgE (see Chapter I), but the outcome of exposure is the same: an asthma attack. Appendix 1 lists foods and drugs containing sulfites. Drugs and other products containing aspirin are listed in Appendix 2.

While most asthma attacks are due to exposure to an allergen, other common triggers include exercise, emotional stress (including pleasurable excitement) and any one of the following environmental irritants:

- Air pollution
- Cigarette smoke and the smell of dirty ashtrays

- Fumes from paint, gasoline, cleaning products
- Fragrances from perfumes, cologne and/or cosmetics
- Cold weather, changes in the weather
- Cooking odors
- Smoking fires, smoking fireplaces
- Steam

Whatever the cause, asthma usually can be managed successfully with good medical treatment. It is true that between one third and one half of all children with asthma eventually "outgrow" the disorder. This is most likely to happen among youngsters who develop asthma between ages two and eight and least likely among those affected before the age of two. Despite this general rule, only time will tell whether any individual child will outgrow asthma, although some doctors believe that proper treatment improves the odds. When youngsters do outgrow asthma, it usually occurs at puberty. Hormonal changes may play a role, but it may also be that the increased size of the airways and bronchial system that comes with physical growth makes obstruction less likely. In that case, the youngsters still have asthma, but their mature anatomy makes them less susceptible to attacks.

INCIDENCE

More than 10 million Americans suffer from asthma, and many of them are also afflicted with hay fever (see Chapter II). Of that total, approximately 3 million asthmatics are children under eighteen. Results of a study completed in 1990 show that the rate of asthma is twice as high among the children of mothers who smoke at least half a pack of cigarettes per day than it is among other youngsters, and that these children are four times as likely to use asthma medication as the asthmatic children of mothers who do not smoke. The incidence of asthma and asthma-related deaths has been increasing in recent years, probably due to both allergic and non-allergic reactions to air pollution. The increase is most marked among young black boys living in the inner cities. Asthma is responsible for some four thousand deaths per year. Most occur among patients over fifty, but children under nine are also at increased risk, particularly those who live in urban areas.

THE MECHANICS OF BREATHING

Asthma is a disorder of the airways, the route air follows from the nose or mouth to the lungs. After it is inhaled, air travels through the larynx or voice box down the trachea or windpipe, which divides into two *bronchi,* tubes that branch right and left toward each of the lungs. If you look at a picture of the bronchial system, the whole apparatus looks like an upside-down tree with the windpipe as the trunk and the bronchi as the main branches off of which smaller and smaller branches reach out through the lungs. At the end of the smaller branches are the *alveoli,* tiny air sacs that look like leaves on the upside-down tree. The exchange of oxygen from inhaled air for carbon dioxide from circulated blood takes place in the blood vessels surrounding the alveoli. Contraction and relaxation of the airways to the alveoli is regulated by smooth muscle.

AN ASTHMA ATTACK

During an asthma attack, the inside lining of the bronchial tubes swells and the muscles surrounding them contract, exerting pressure that narrows the airspace. To make matters worse, mucus production increases, leading to the formation of thick, sticky mucus that can harden and form plugs that block the tubes. The cumulative effect of this obstruction makes it very difficult to exhale, leading to some or all of the following symptoms:

- Tightness in the chest
- Shortness of breath
- Coughing
- Wheezing
- Anxiety
- Thick mucus

Less common symptoms include rapid heartbeat, restlessness, pallor, fatigue, vomiting and postnasal drip.

Asthma attacks can develop suddenly, but most patients experience warning signs, sometimes a day in advance. These signs may be subtle and may differ from person to person. Breathing changes are the most common warnings, but a wide range of physical symptoms and mood or behavioral changes can occur. By learning to recognize them, you can take steps to head off the attack or, at least, reduce its severity. Parents of asthmatic children should take note of the complaints, breathing and behavior changes that signal an approaching attack. Among them:

- Coughing
- Shortness of breath
- Tightness in the chest
- Breathing through the mouth
- Increased pulse rate
- Fatigue
- Itching at the back of the throat
- Not feeling well
- Nervousness
- Irritability
- Easily upset

In addition to these symptoms, children may become overactive or unusually quiet. Less common signs of an impending attack can be perspiration, pallor, a reddened or swollen face, dark circles under the eyes, flared nostrils.

Most asthma attacks subside on their own or in response to medication. Those that continue or worsen despite treatment are known as *status asthmaticus,* and require emergency medical attention. The following symptoms indicate that an emergency is developing:

- Labored breathing
- Breathing from the neck up
- Perspiration
- Flared nostrils
- Raised shoulders
- Indentation at hollow of the neck
- Fearfulness
- Holding hands over the head

• Lips and fingernail beds turn blue. *This is an indication of cyanosis, a lack of oxygen.*

Should any or all of these symptoms develop, call the doctor immediately and/or go to the nearest hospital emergency room.

ASTHMA AND EMOTIONS

A persistent myth holds that asthma is an emotional, not a physical, disorder, stemming from childhood maladjustment or an unhealthy relationship between mother and child. Another long-standing myth maintains that victims can bring on attacks at will. While it is true that emotions can play a role in many diseases, including asthma, there is no medical basis for the belief that emotional factors actually *cause* asthma or that attacks can be "willed" into happening. A victim's emotions or emotional state *can* lead to reckless or careless exposure to an allergen that can trigger an attack. And, of course, an unhealthy parent-child relationship can develop as a result of or even precede a child's asthma. This may be due to a tendency to overprotect an asthmatic child or to other, unrelated factors. In neither case is the quality of the relationship the *cause* of the asthma itself.

However, there is little doubt that psychological stress can contribute to asthma attacks and worsen an attack in progress. Victims, particularly children, can become very anxious if not hysterical as an uncontrolled attack progresses and breathing becomes more and more difficult.

It is also true that asthma can give rise to emotional and psychological problems. Asthmatics may be afraid to travel, fearful of being alone during life-threatening attacks, severely embarrassed when attacks occur in public. Particularly among children, the need for treatment and the unpredictability of attacks can set them apart. As a result, some youngsters become self-conscious and/or fearful. Parents and doctors can help them overcome these natural reactions with reassurance and optimism. Parents may have to temper an inclination to overprotect an asthmatic child. While good care requires some precautions, most youngsters can live normal lives and be as active as their peers.

DIAGNOSIS

A number of other disorders can cause asthmalike symptoms. These include:
- Chronic bronchitis, a condition that usually affects longtime cigarette smokers
- Emphysema, a progressive lung disorder that causes shortness of breath and usually affects smokers.
- Heart failure, a condition stemming from an impairment in the heart's ability to pump blood.

In children, bronchitis, croup and pneumonia can cause wheezing that may be mistaken for asthma. Obstruction from swallowing a small object can also cause wheezing in children. If this develops suddenly, it indicates that a child has swallowed something that is interfering with breathing. *This is an emergency requiring immediate medical treatment.*

Certain anatomical abnormalities of the trachea can also bring on asthmatic symptoms in young children. Some of these are outgrown; others may require surgical correction.

In order to confirm that symptoms are due to asthma and not some other condition, one or more of the medical tests described below may be required. In addition, you may need allergy testing, described in Chapter VII.

Spirometry

This test is designed to determine if the airways are obstructed. Patients are required to take a deep breath and then exhale as completely as possible into the mouthpiece of a mechanical device called a *spirometer*. To make sure that all the exhaled air is captured, patients must wear a nose clip and a tightly fitting mouthpiece. The volume of air expelled is measured against the total amount of air the lungs can normally hold. (This is individually determined, taking into consideration age, height, weight and sex.) If the test reveals that lung capacity is less than 80 percent of normal, it is repeated after administration of a bronchodilator, a drug that can open obstructed airways. If results are then normal, asthma is the problem, since these drugs don't affect any of the other conditions that can obstruct the airways.

Bronchial Provocation Tests

This is a variation on spirometry that makes use of drugs to trigger asthmatic breathing among patients who complain of asthmalike symptoms but have normal spirometry results. The patient inhales the drug methacholine or histamine, both of which can bring on wheezing among asthmatics but do not affect nonasthmatics, whether or not they have another lung condition. The spirometry is then repeated.

Two other tests may be required under special circumstances:

CHEST X RAY: This procedure can diagnose fractured ribs or pneumonia. Rib fractures can occur during a severe asthma attack, and asthmatics are more susceptible than normal to respiratory infections, including pneumonia.

ARTERIAL BLOOD GAS: This test measures levels of oxygen or carbon dioxide in the bloodstream. The less oxygen and more carbon dioxide, the greater the danger of respiratory failure. Arterial blood-gas studies usually are ordered during an acute attack being treated in a hospital emergency room.

BREATHING EXERCISES

Breathing exercises can help lessen the anxiety that often accompanies an asthma attack and can reduce the severity of the attack. If you have not been taught breathing exercises, ask your doctor about them before attempting them on your own. (See the Resources section on page 113 for a list of organizations that publish and/or distribute information on breathing and breathing exercises for asthmatics.) The exercise that follows is an example of the type of breathing exercise often recommended for asthma patients:

- Sit in a comfortable straight-backed chair, feet flat on the floor.
- Place one hand on the diaphragm (below your ribs) and the other on your chest.
- Inhale slowly through your nose. The hand on your diaphragm should move out, the one on your chest should not move at all.

Exhale slowly through the mouth. The hand on your diaphragm moves in; the one on your chest remains still.

LIVING WITH ASTHMA

When asthma is due to allergy, the most effective treatment is to reduce or eliminate exposure to the allergen. Dust and pollen are the allergens most frequently responsible (see Chapter II, which also describes methods for eliminating or reducing exposure).

Not everyone with asthma needs to use one, but when early signs of an impending attack occur, a device called a *peak-flow meter* can indicate whether the ability to exhale is diminishing. The meter allows you to compare the amount of air you can exhale at any given time to the amount you can exhale when breathing is unobstructed. You simply exhale three hard breaths in succession into the mouthpiece of the *spirometer* (also called a huffer). Space the breaths about fifteen seconds apart and compare the highest reading to your normal level. If it is low, you might take medication prescribed to prevent an attack or call your doctor for advice. Some people test themselves with home peak-flow meters twice a day.

Once early warning signs appear, the following steps can head off an attack:

- *Stop what you are doing and relax.* If you do breathing exercises, begin them now.
- *Drink liquids.* Warm beverages are best. They replace fluids in the airways that evaporate as breathing changes. They thin and help expel the thick mucus that forms during an attack. They help relax the airways. Tea, coffee, clear soup, warm cider are all appropriate. If warm liquids aren't available, cold ones will do. Drink as much as possible, at least eight ounces every half hour.
- *Take your medications.* Consult Chapter IX for details.

A number of drugs can effectively control asthma and reverse attacks. They fall into the following general categories:

- *Bronchodilators,* including xanthines, which relieve symptoms by relaxing the muscles surrounding the airways; and adrenergic drugs, which act on nerve cells in the bronchial system. The choice of bronchodilator depends on the frequency and severity of attacks.
- *Cromolyn sodium* treats asthma by preventing allergic reactions from occurring; it may take a

month or two of treatment before improvement becomes noticeable.

- *Corticosteroids* are powerful drugs that reduce inflammation and may stimulate production of cyclic AMP, a body chemical that relaxes bronchial muscles. They are powerful drugs that can have serious side effects, including weight gain and, in children, temporary suppression of normal growth.
- *Antihistamines* can control allergic rhinitis among affected asthmatics.

Some of these drugs can be taken by mouth, but many must be inhaled. This requires use of devices that dispense medication. Some are electrically powered machines called nebulizers that create a fine mist by combining the drug with a liquid saline (salt) solution; others are handheld portable devices called metered-dose inhalers that deliver the medication into the mouth. While convenient, the portable inhalers may invite overuse, which can worsen rather than relieve asthma symptoms. An increase in asthma deaths among children with asthma in Great Britain was due to overuse of these devices. Although the drugs used in Britain at the time were stronger than those available in the United States, many physicians are still reluctant to prescribe handheld inhalers, particularly for children. Others note that there are fewer drug side effects when medication is taken via these devices and that more asthma deaths are due to underuse rather than overuse of medication.

The handheld devices are very convenient. They permit increased mobility among asthmatics, and reduce the fear of suffering an unanticipated attack. For example, asthmatics allergic to animals can pretreat themselves with a bronchodilator administered via a handheld nebulizer when visiting friends or relatives with pets or before exercise if they are susceptible to exercise-induced attacks.

EXERCISE-INDUCED ASTHMA

Up to 90 percent of all people with asthma are susceptible to attacks brought on by exercise. This condition, exercise-induced asthma (EIA), also affects about 40 percent of children with allergic rhinitis (see Chapter II) and can develop among people who are not otherwise susceptible to asthma.

Attacks usually occur five to ten minutes after, not during, exercise, though some delayed reactions develop hours later. Most are brief and subside within minutes, but they can continue for up to two hours and may require treatment with a bronchodilator.

Symptoms can range from coughing to tightness in the chest, wheezing and shortness of breath. Young children may complain of stomach cramps, and some people report headaches, which are probably related to an underlying sinus condition or nasal congestion.

Causes

Only vigorous and prolonged physical activity can trigger asthma symptoms. As a general rule, an attack will not occur unless the exercise is strenuous enough to raise an adult's heart rate to 150 beats per minute and a child's to 170. Running, jogging and cold-weather sports such as ice hockey and skiing are most likely to provoke an attack of exercise-induced asthma among susceptible people. The problem is not the effort involved. Instead, the attacks appear to stem from loss of heat and moisture from tissues lining the respiratory tract. This can occur as a result of inhaling large amounts of air, particularly cold, dry air. The fact that swimming is unlikely to trigger exercise-induced asthma may stem from the fact that the air inhaled by swimmers is warm and moist.

There is also the possibility that exercise somehow triggers an allergic reaction that brings on the asthma attack. Researchers have found high blood levels of histamine and other chemical mediators of allergy (see Chapter I) in people with EIA. The irritating effects of heat and water loss on tissues lining the respiratory tract might be responsible for the reaction.

Treatment

Troublesome as EIA may be, avoiding exercise is not the solution to the problem. Indeed, today's approach to asthma treatment emphasizes the benefits of exercise for all but the most severely affected patients. That means encouraging youngsters with asthma to participate in games and sports even if they need medication to prevent or treat attacks of asthma. The same holds true for adults and athletes, regardless of age. However, anyone susceptible to exercise-induced asthma should avoid or cut back on exercise under the following conditions:

- Bad air pollution (sulfur-dioxide levels of 0.5 parts per million; ozone levels of 0.9 parts per million)
- Very cold weather (temperatures significantly lower than those you are accustomed to)
- A high pollen count
- A respiratory-tract infection

MEDICATIONS: Certain drugs can reduce the likelihood of an EIA attack. They include the adrenergic bronchodilators albuterol, metaproterenol and terbutaline taken thirty minutes before exercise; cromolyn sodium taken before can prevent attacks but won't affect symptoms once an attack is under way; theophylline is also useful but isn't ideal because it doesn't become fully effective in some people until an hour or two after it is taken. For this reason, timing can be a problem—some patients may forget to take it on time. All of these antiasthma drugs are acceptable under Olympic rules for athletic competition. (See Chapter IX for information on dosage, administration and side effects.)

Should symptoms develop, a few minutes' rest will usually bring them under control; if not, two inhalations of a bronchodilator is usually effective.

CHAPTER IV

FOOD AND DRUG ALLERGIES

OF all allergies, those involving foods or drugs would seem to be the simplest to identify and control. But determining whether an adverse reaction to a food or drug is caused by allergy or something else is not easy. From a practical point of view, it may not matter at all whether a food or drug makes you sick because you're allergic to it or because of some nonallergic problem. Since there is no treatment for food allergy other than avoiding the food in question and only a temporary means of overcoming drug allergy, confirming that an allergy is to blame for symptoms may not seem important.

In some cases, it isn't. However, many people erroneously attribute a wide variety of symptoms to allergies to foods, food additives or other chemicals that might be loosely classified as drugs. As a result, they needlessly limit their diets and life-styles. It is important to avoid a food or drug that triggers an adverse reaction, but it is equally important to recognize and understand that a number of other factors might explain these reactions, including the possibility that symptoms may be triggered by the mistaken *belief* that an allergy exists. Some tests have shown that these psychosomatic reactions are more common than true food allergies.

FOOD ALLERGIES

While many people experience unpleasant and sometimes dangerous reactions to food, upon investigation relatively few of those reactions turn out to be "true" food allergies. As explained in Chapter I, an allergy involves production of IgE antibodies that set off symptoms in the presence of a specific allergen. These reactions are relatively rare. It is estimated that between 3 and 7 percent of the population suffers from true food allergies. Most cases occur among children, the majority of whom outgrow their allergies. The most susceptible youngsters are those whose parents have allergies, though not necessarily food allergies. Some allergies to cow's milk that begin in infancy are due to the immaturity of the digestive tract. When this is the case, the babies can outgrow their sensitivities in a matter of weeks.

"True" food-allergy symptoms typically affect the gastrointestinal tract, although skin reactions such as hives, eczema, asthma and rhinitis also can occur. The most dangerous reaction is anaphylactic shock, a constellation of severe symptoms that can be fatal and require prompt emergency treatment. (See page xlvii in the Emergencies section for a full description.)

You don't have to be allergic to a food to suffer symptoms when you eat it. Any one of the following problems may cause an adverse reaction:

FOOD IDIOSYNCRACIES: These reactions can occur among people with a certain predisposition that permits *symptoms* to develop. For example, some asthma patients develop attacks in response to sulfites used in some foods as preservatives or bleaching agents. This reaction (see Chapter III) is limited to asthmatics, although relatively few of them are sulfite-sensitive.

A few years ago some studies seemed to indicate that hyperactivity among children was sometimes an idiosyncratic reaction to artificial food colorings and flavorings. This thesis has not subsequently been substantiated. Nor has the theory that sugar contributes to aggressive behavior in children. There are, however, some scientists who continue to explore these possibilities.

Food idiosyncracies may be to blame for some headaches in people prone to migraines and could play a role in some cases of irritable-bowel syndrome, a disorder that can cause gastrointestinal distress, including diarrhea and constipation. However, no direct correlation has been shown to indicate that foods actually cause either of these conditions.

METABOLIC REACTIONS: Two food-related disorders are due to inborn disturbances in metabolism. The best known is *lactose intolerance,* which stems from the deficiency of the enzyme lactase, needed to digest lactose, a sugar in milk and other dairy products. Symptoms are gas and diarrhea. Up to 90 percent of all blacks and Orientals are affected, and the incidence is also high among Jews, Arabs and Greeks. Lactose intolerance occurs among less than 12 percent of other Caucasians. Prevalence increases with age. The only treatment is to limit consumption of dairy products although yogurt and acidophilus milk are often well tolerated.

CELIAC DISEASE: This disorder causes diarrhea and bloating in response to foods containing gluten, a protein in wheat, rye, barley and oats. Symptoms may also include weight loss, fatigue, weakness and sometimes anemia and bone pain due to lack of absorption of iron and calcium, respectively. No one knows for sure if celiac disease is really a metabolic disorder, although it certainly isn't an allergy. It may stem from damage to certain cells in the small intestine, but exactly how this damage occurs has not yet been determined. The only way to confirm a diagnosis is with an intestinal biopsy. The disorder can begin at any age. Treatment requires avoiding all gluten-containing grains, a tricky enterprise since many prepared foods contain "hidden" grains.

FOOD POISONING: Due to bacterial, viral or parasitic contamination of food, this condition's symptoms include vomiting, nausea and stomach cramps that usually subside within twenty-four hours.

In addition to the disorders described above, symptoms that appear to be food-related may be due to any one of a number of gastrointestinal diseases. Stress and emotional problems can also affect the digestive system, causing symptoms that may be mistakenly attributed to food.

THE REAL THING

True food allergies usually cause symptoms that become apparent immediately upon eating the food responsible, although delays of several hours are possible. Most reactions involve the gastrointestinal tract. Symptoms can begin when the offending food comes in contact with the mouth. They include:

- Itching of the lips and mouth.
- Nausea
- Vomiting
- Diarrhea
- Stomach ache or cramps
- Rectal itching
- Colic (in infants)

Food allergies can also affect the skin, causing any one of the reactions described below and more extensively in Chapter V.

HIVES: Hives form as a result of enlarged and leaking small blood vessels in the outer layers of skin. These itchy skin eruptions can be allergic or nonallergic in nature. Some people get them for no known reason.

ANGIOEDEMA: Similar to hives, this condition occurs in deeper layers of skin. The most severe form, hereditary angioedema, is caused by the absence of a blood protein and is unrelated to allergy. Angioedema can cause swelling in the tongue or throat.

ECZEMA: This red, crusty rash occurs in patches, usually on the cheeks, but can spread to the neck, arms, legs and trunk. It itches constantly. Eczema is almost always an allergic reaction to foods, often eggs, milk and peanuts. It tends to develop early in life, usually in infancy.

Asthma attacks can also develop as a consequence of food allergy, and recent studies suggest that allergies to foods underlie perennial allergic rhinitis much more often than once thought.

Some migraine headaches appear to be associated with true food allergies, but the connection between food and migraines has been verified in only a few cases.

Seasonal Food Allergies

Some food-allergy symptoms appear seasonally. There are two explanations for this phenomenon:

- Certain foods may be consumed in greater quantity when they are most plentiful. Thus, a mild allergy that causes no trouble ordinarily could flare up when you eat more than you're accustomed to of the food responsible.
- People with seasonal allergies like hay fever may also then be supersensitive to foods that ordinarily don't trouble them.

COMMON FOOD ALLERGENS

Although any food can cause an allergic reaction, those listed below are most often responsible:

- Cow's milk
- Eggs

- Nuts
- Whitefish
- Shellfish
- Soy beans and soybean-based products
- Wheat
- Corn
- Bananas
- Chicken
- Melons
- Grains including wheat and corn. (A recent study at Johns Hopkins School of Medicine suggests that contrary to common belief, grain allergies are so rare that patients should not be asked to eliminate wheat from their diets without definite proof that they are allergic.)

In rare instances, someone who is allergic to one food turns out to be sensitive to another that is closely related biologically such as lemons and oranges, both citrus fruits. See Appendix 4 for a list of related foods.

Allergy to cow's milk is generally more common among children than adults. Youngsters usually outgrow the problem before puberty. Adults are prone to allergies to seafood, including both shellfish (shrimp, crabs, lobsters, clams, oysters, scallops and mussels) and other types of fish. People who are allergic to fish usually react to a single species, not all types of fish.

With rare exceptions, the following foods are *unlikely* to cause allergies:

Fruits: Apples (and apple juice), grape juice, peaches, pears, plums

Meats: Beef, lamb, turkey
Vegetables: Beets, carrots, lettuce, potatoes, rice, squash, sweet potatoes
Grains: Barley, oats, rye
Others: Salt, tea

DIAGNOSIS

Diagnosing food allergy can be relatively straightforward if you suspect that a particular food is responsible, and extremely difficult if you don't know what is causing the trouble or if symptoms are delayed rather than immediate. Whatever the case, the process begins with keeping a food diary (see page xxxii), a detailed record of everything you eat for a week to ten days and of any symptoms that develop during that period.

The next step may be an elimination diet (see Appendix 3). Under a doctor's supervision, you cut out foods that appear to be responsible to see if symptoms disappear. If they do, you reintroduce the foods one at a time in a doctor's office. If symptoms reappear after introducing a particular food, you have probably found the culprit. However, results can be confused by several factors: the amount you eat, the way the food is prepared, medications you are taking, other foods eaten at the same time that may affect digestion.

Allergy tests aren't particularly helpful in diagnosing food allergies. Skin tests (see Chapter VIII) can produce a positive response to a food that causes no symptoms at all when eaten. However, a negative skin test usually rules out the food in question. For example,

if you are being tested for an allergy to peanuts
skin-test results show that you're not allergic
them, it is unlikely that peanuts are the source of your
problem.

Blood tests for the presence of IgE antibodies to various foods aren't sensitive enough to establish the presence of a food allergy. However, RAST tests (see
Chapter VIII) may be used when eczema is so severe
that it would interfere with testing or when skin testing
might provoke an anaphylactic reaction.

The gold standard of food-allergy testing is the
double-blind challenge. Patients are given two capsules
or liquids, one of which contains an extract of a food
suspected of causing the allergic reaction; the other
contains no active ingredients. Two challenges are performed each day. Neither the doctor nor the patient
knows which is which (someone uninvolved in the test
keeps the records). The blind nature of the test prevents
any bias on the part of either patient or doctor from
influencing the outcome. If no reaction occurs, the suspected food cannot be to blame for the allergic symptoms. This test can't be used for patients with
anaphylactic reactions to food.

TREATMENT

The only treatment for food allergy is to avoid the food
that causes the reaction. Depending on what that food
is, this task may not be as simple as it sounds. If you
are allergic to eggs, for instance, you have to avoid all
foods that contain eggs. This means scrutinizing the la-

bels of prepared foods and carefully questioning waiters in restaurants to make sure that the food you're allergic to isn't used as an ingredient in whatever dish you want to order. Recent studies have found that even foods labeled "non-dairy" can contain amounts of milk that, while very small, can cause a reaction among those allergic to milk. Bear in mind, too, that because milk-derived products are classified as "natural flavoring" by the U.S. Department of Agriculture, manufacturers are not required to list them on labels. A tiny amount of milk in a hot dog can set off a reaction in a child highly allergic to milk.

The severity of your allergy will determine how careful you must be. If you have had an anaphylactic reaction in the past, letting down your guard can cost you your life. One young woman with a severe allergy to peanuts died in the course of an anaphylactic reaction to chili containing peanut butter. It probably never occurred to her to ask whether peanuts were among the ingredients, but these days no combination of foods is beyond the imagination of creative chefs. You can't be too careful. And bear in mind that with severe food allergies, reactions can be set off by the aroma of food and even by kissing someone who has recently eaten the food to which you are allergic. As a precaution, anyone highly allergic to any food, no matter how seldom encountered, should always carry injectable epinephrine for use should a reaction occur. (See the Emergencies section on page xlvii for a review of injection instructions.)

With allergies that cause less severe symptoms, the foods responsible may be reintroduced eventually under a doctor's supervision. If no reaction occurs, it migh. be possible to eat small amounts occasionally, although there will always be the danger that in time the full-fledged allergy will recur.

Some doctors suggest that food allergies can be prevented from developing among babies of allergic parents by breast-feeding them during infancy, and others urge nursing mothers with a family history of allergies to avoid eating highly allergenic foods. It may also be prudent to withhold allergenic foods from babies with a strong family history of allergies until they reach their first birthday. However, there is no guarantee that any of these tactics will work.

Neither drugs used to treat other types of allergies nor immunotherapy (see Chapter IX) is useful in treating food allergies.

DRUG ALLERGIES

Adverse reactions to drugs are not unusual, but confirming that allergy is responsible is sometimes difficult. Studies have shown that drug allergies may affect between 3 to 35 percent of the population. In order to develop a drug allergy, your body must first be sensitized to the drug. Then, once an adverse reaction occurs, symptoms appear on subsequent exposure. For example, if you're allergic to penicillin, you probably took penicillin at least once without incident. Your allergy symptoms appeared the next time penicillin was prescribed and will probably continue.

Observations of drug allergies have led to a few general conclusions about their nature:

- You are more likely to develop an allergy to a drug you take occasionally than one you take continuously.
- Drugs taken by mouth are less likely to provoke an allergic reaction than drugs injected or applied to the skin.
- Children and the elderly are less susceptible to drug allergies than others. This is probably because of the immaturity of the immune system in youngsters and the fact that as we age, the immune system becomes less reactive.
- The risk of drug allergy is higher in the presence of tissue injury or intestinal, kidney or liver damage which can alter the way the body handles medication.

NONALLERGIC REACTIONS

Before a drug allergy can be blamed for an adverse reaction, a number of other possibilities must be considered. They include:

PSEUDOALLERGIC REACTIONS: In these reactions, the symptoms are the same as those caused by drug allergy. However, the IgE scenario (see Chapter I) that occurs when allergy is present does not occur. The most common pseudoallergic drug reaction involves aspirin and affects about 1 million Americans. The group most susceptible to these reactions are people with chronic hives, hay fever and asthma. Avoiding aspirin and drugs containing aspirin (see Appendix 2 for a list) is the only treatment. Some people who are aspirin-sensitive also react to tartrazine (a yellow food coloring), drugs containing ibuprofen, the food preservative sodium benzoate and the drugs indomethacin (for arthritis), mefenamic acid (an anti-inflammatory), phenylbutazone (for arthritis).

The antibiotic ampicillin causes a pseudoallergic rash in 9 percent of all people who take it and in half of all patients with infectious mononucleosis.

Contrast dyes injected for some X rays cause any one of several allergy-like symptoms (including hives, itching, rashes, asthma attacks or even anaphylactic shock) in about 3 percent of all patients. New tests that don't require contrast-dye injection often can be substituted for X rays in susceptible patients.

IDIOSYNCRATIC REACTIONS: These are unexpected and unusual reactions to certain drugs. Examples include ringing in the ears after taking quinine, or reduced production of blood cells while taking the antibiotic chloramphenicol.

PARADOXICAL REACTIONS: Those responses cause symptoms that are the opposite of the expected effect of a drug. Nervousness or agitation after taking a tranquilizer would constitute a paradoxical drug reaction. These occur most often among children and the elderly.

SIDE EFFECTS: All drugs produce some undesirable side effects. One of the most common examples is the drowsiness caused by some antihistamines. Some drug side effects include rashes and other symptoms that might be mistaken for an allergic reaction.

OVERDOSE: Taking too much of any medication, even

a nonprescription drug, can bring on a wide variety of symptoms, some quite dangerous.

DRUG INTERACTIONS: The combined effect of two or more drugs can bring on adverse reactions. If you think you are allergic to a drug, be sure to tell the doctor about everything you are taking or using, prescription or nonprescription. This includes aspirin, antihistamines, laxatives, nose drops, birth-control pills, cold remedies and cough medicines, vitamins, medicated skin lotions or ointments and anything else you are using for any purpose. Since alcohol can play a role in drug-related reactions, be sure to ask the doctor if drinking could be a factor.

SYMPTOMS

Drug allergies can cause reactions affecting the skin, lungs, internal organs such as the liver and kidneys, the blood vessels and many different tissues throughout the body. Among them:

ANAPHYLACTIC SHOCK, discussed in Chapter I, usually appears within an hour after taking the allergenic drug and requires prompt emergency action (See the Emergencies section on page xlvii).

SKIN: The easiest allergies to detect are those involving the skin. Hives, rashes, itching, swelling can all indicate the presence of allergy, but they also can be signs of a drug side effect or symptoms of the illness the drug is being used to treat.

RESPIRATORY SYSTEM: When the lungs are affected, a

drug allergy can cause an asthma attack, wheezing, laryngeal symptoms, coughing, rhinorrhea or an inflammation of the membranes lining the lung.

INTERNAL ORGANS: Symptoms involving internal organs may take months to develop. They include hepatitis (a liver disorder), nephritis (kidney inflammation), abnormal bleeding and damage to white blood cells that can affect resistance to infection. If the allergy responsible isn't detected and drug treatment is stopped, the damaging effects can worsen.

DRUG FEVER: Fever as a drug reaction is usually but not always due to allergy. It usually occurs a week or ten days after a drug treatment begins, but can begin within an hour or two after taking the first dose. The fever can be very low or very high, constant or intermittent, and may be accompanied by other symptoms, including rash, hives, painful and/or swollen joints, swollen glands, hepatitis or hemolytic anemia. The fever usually subsides once treatment stops.

COMMON DRUG ALLERGIES

Any drug can cause an allergy, but penicillin and other antibiotics are frequent culprits. Diabetics can become allergic to certain forms of insulin.

PENICILLIN: One in every fifty people treated with penicillin develops some type of allergic response. Most of these (76 percent) are skin reactions (hives, rashes); 22 percent involve fever, serum sickness, asthma attacks, angioedema or vasculitis; 2 percent of those allergic to penicillin develop anaphylactic shock. Symptoms usually develop soon after treatment starts, but can occur up to a week later.

The seriousness of the reaction depends on whether a major or minor penicillin breakdown product causes the allergy. Skin tests can identify which is responsible. An allergy to the major determinant usually means that you'll get hives soon after you take penicillin; an allergy to the minor determinant indicates that taking penicillin could bring on anaphylactic shock.

NEOMYCIN: An allergy to this antibiotic can cause pink eye (conjunctivitis) if the drug is in eyedrops or contact dermatitis if neomycin is in ointments used to treat skin conditions.

STREPTOMYCIN, CHLORAMPHENICOL AND SULFA DRUGS: All of these have been associated with allergic reactions, including anaphylactic shock.

INSULIN: Most insulin allergies cause short-lived skin reactions at the site of the injection, although more severe responses, including anaphylactic shock, are possible. Switching from pork or beef insulin to human insulin or more purified types of animal insulin usually solves the problem.

INSECT-STING
ALLERGIES

▼

ALLERGIES to insect stings affect up to 3 percent of the population although as much as 30 percent may have a positive response to skin tests. Like other allergies, these develop only after you have been sensitized. With insect stings, this means that you must have been stung at least once before by the same type of insect. As a result of the previous sting or stings, you develop IgE antibodies to the insect's venom, which set off the reaction the next time you are stung.

Insect-sting allergies are somewhat unique. Unlike other allergies, they are not inherited. You need not have a personal or family history of allergies to be affected. No one knows why some people are susceptible and others are not. Many people first learn they have an insect-sting allergy from a life-threatening reaction. Symptoms of anaphylactic shock, the most severe outcome of an insect sting, include a rapid outbreak of hives, swelling of the lips, ears, eyelids, palms and soles of the feet, nausea, diarrhea or stomach cramps, breathing difficulties, dizziness, a drop in blood pressure. An injection of the drug epinephrine can reverse anaphylaxis. At least fifty deaths per year stem from these reactions, although the number may be much higher. Of course, not all insect-sting allergies have such dangerous and dramatic consequences. In some cases, even severe allergies are only temporary.

BAD BUGS

The stinging insects responsible for most allergies in the United States belong to the order Hymenoptera. Here is a rundown:

Honeybee

- Not aggressive unless provoked
- Most common of the stinging insects
- Hairy body with bright yellow or black markings
- Found around flowers, clover
- Leaves a stinger with a white venom sac. (If you can scrape or flick the stinger off the skin with a fingernail, you may be able to avoid or reduce the severity of a reaction. Don't squeeze it—by doing so, you may force more venom into the skin.)
- Nests usually are in commercial hives
- Dies after stinging

Yellow Jackets

- Most aggressive of stinging insects
- Bright yellow and black markings

- Strongly attracted to sugar and foods containing sugar (including juices and other sweet drinks)
- Found around garbage cans, picnics, exposed food
- Nests are large and round and made of a combination of rotted wood, stems, leaves, paper and cardboard that insects have chewed; built in the ground, on compost heaps, piles of timber.
- Can and will sting repeatedly

Hornets

- Black with yellow or white markings
- Short body
- Nests are oval, found in trees or bushes
- Can and will sting repeatedly

Wasp

- Hairless, black, brown or red
- Narrow "waist" separates chest from long, slim lower body
- Nests are horizontal combs of paper cells; underside is exposed; found under eaves and rafters
- Can and will sting repeatedly

Stinging ants, particularly the fire ant of the southeast, are also troublemakers. They are nasty, aggressive little creatures that get their name from the fact that normally their attacks cause an intense burning sensation. Allergic reactions include anaphylactic shock.

Whether you're allergic or not, it is never a good idea to disturb a stinging insect's nest. If you find one on your property, have an exterminator remove it. Don't try to burn or flood it. You will only make the insects angry and endanger yourself.

THE STING

Insect stings cause the following reactions:

NORMAL (NONALLERGIC) LOCAL REACTION: A burning sensation, swelling and redness at the site of the sting. Symptoms appear soon after the sting and usually subside within an hour even without treatment, and disappear within a day. You can reduce the swelling and relieve the sting with ice or cold compresses.

LARGE LOCAL REACTIONS: More severe swelling and redness in the area of the sting. These may take several hours to develop and may continue to cause swelling and discomfort for a week or more. An example would be a sting on the cheek that causes swelling and discomfort in the lips and eyelids. Antihistamines or corticosteroids may be prescribed to bring down the swelling.

TOXIC REACTION: The result of multiple stings; symptoms can occur throughout the body and may include nausea, diarrhea, breathing difficulties, dizziness and shock. Symptoms usually develop immediately after a person is stung. They require immediate medical attention and treatment with epinephrine.

SYSTEMIC: Symptoms appear soon after the sting, occur far from the site of the sting, and can include any and all of the signs of anaphylactic shock described above. If you are bitten on the arm and develop hives all over your body or any symptoms at all anywhere beyond the site of the sting, you are having a systemic reaction.

DIAGNOSIS

Establishing that a reaction to an insect sting was allergic, and therefore amenable to treatment, requires more than a description of the symptoms. You also have to know what type of insect stung you, and for treatment to make sense, your reaction must have been severe enough to warrant the time, trouble and expense.

Skin testing (see Chapter VII) can identify the allergen, in this case the specific venom. For most accurate results, tests should be done at least three or four weeks after a reaction has occurred. There is a possibility of a false-negative reaction if tests are performed sooner. This means that results could be negative when allergy is present.

Testing does present some risk of a reaction to the venom used. For this reason, some doctors prefer blood tests (see RAST testing, Chapter VII) to confirm allergy, though they are less reliable than skin testing. Between 15 and 20 percent of these tests miss finding the allergies.

PREVENTION

As with other allergies, the best form of treatment is avoidance:

- Stay away from areas that attract insects. These include garbage and trash cans, gardens, picnic grounds.
- Keep garage areas and patios clean.
- Don't walk barefoot out of doors.
- Be careful when mowing the lawn, clipping hedges; if possible, assign these chores to someone else.
- If dining out of doors, keep food covered until you are ready to eat, and re-cover after food is served.
- Avoid perfume, scented hair spray, deodorant, cosmetics and other fragrances; the smell attracts insects.
- Avoid loose-fitting clothes; insects can become trapped in filmy garments.
- Cover as much of your body as possible when spending time out of doors, particularly in the late summer and early fall when insects are out and about.
- Wear light-colored clothing; bright colors, vivid prints and black attract insects.
- Keep a can of insecticide in the car; keep the car windows closed as much as possible, and check to make sure no insects are in the car before you enter.
- Don't engage in outdoor activities alone; you may need help if stung.
- Wear Medic-Alert identification stating that you are allergic to insect stings. (See page xlvii for information on obtaining Medic-Alert tags or bracelets.)

TREATMENT

Insect-sting allergies can be controlled and adverse reactions prevented with immunotherapy (see Chapter VIII), a series of allergy shots that build up your resistance to the venom responsible for your reaction. This involves injecting you with purified venom from the insect in question. However, since purified fire-ant extracts are not available, whole-body extracts of stinging insects are used for immunization. Whole-body extracts should not be used against any other insect-sting allergies since the purified venom is more effective. A recent study found that the protection against allergic reactions to stings afforded by allergy shots lasts at least one year after the shots are discontinued.

Immunotherapy for insect-sting allergies is appropriate only for people who have had life-threatening reactions in the past and have tested positive to one of the insect venoms. It is not effective against large local reactions or toxic reactions.

EMERGENCIES

A systemic reaction to an insect sting requires prompt action:

- If you have had a similar reaction before, your doctor may have prescribed an emergency insect-sting kit containing injectable epinephrine. Use it.
- Then get help and go to your doctor's office or the nearest hospital emergency room. Depending on

the severity of your reaction, you may need further treatment.

- If you don't have an emergency kit, get help and go to the nearest hospital or your doctor's office immediately after being stung.

Here's a checklist to follow if you do have an Emergency Insect-Sting Kit:

- Keep one at home and another at work or school.
- Make sure the expiration date has not passed.
- Store the kit in a cool, dark place; exposure to light can speed deterioration of the drug; the refrigerator is ideal.
- Take the kit with you whenever you travel away from home, particularly if you plan to spend time out of doors.
- Tuck an extra kit into your luggage when traveling so you will always have a spare in case you misplace or use up the first one.
- Make sure that your spouse, parent, teacher and/or traveling companion know(s) where the kit is and how to use it.

ALLERGY
AND THE
SKIN

▼

ALLERGIES can trigger three skin disorders: eczema; hives; and contact dermatitis, a reaction that occurs when susceptible people touch a substance to which they have been sensitized. Poison ivy is the most common type of contact dermatitis. Eczema and hives are often but not always manifestations of an allergy to a food or drug, and also may accompany hay fever or asthma.

You are most likely to develop an allergic skin condition if you have other allergies.

ECZEMA

About 90 percent of all cases of eczema (also known as *atopic dermatitis*) develop during infancy and early childhood, typically before age five. Eczema runs in families and is more common among youngsters with a strong family history of allergy. Both hay fever and asthma occur more frequently than usual among children with eczema. Although about half of all affected youngsters outgrow eczema, often within a year or two, those with asthma, hay fever, or a family history of eczema are less likely to outgrow the disorder.

The first symptom, itching, occurs even before any change in the skin is apparent. A red rash appears next, usually on the cheeks. Other commonly affected areas include the neck, arms and legs, particularly the backs of the elbows and knees and the area behind the ears. In severe cases, "sheets" of thick, purplish rash spread across the body. Scratching the itch spreads the rash and irritates the skin, which then becomes rough, thick and cracked. It may ooze or weep, and when the moisture dries, a crust forms. In this injured condition, the skin is very susceptible to infection. You can easily spot infected areas: Look for unusual redness and draining and swollen glands under the arm or in the groin.

Although children can develop a number of skin conditions, including the familiar diaper rash, eczema is distinguished by its persistent itch and characteristic locations on the body.

Allergy and Eczema

Among children food allergies, usually to eggs, milk, peanuts, soy, wheat or fish are often associated with eczema (see Chapter IV). Because eczema can spread if not treated properly and promptly, it is important to get medical attention as soon as symptoms occur. Don't delay treatment while experimenting with a child's diet to see whether a food allergy is to blame. A physican can readily differentiate eczema from other skin conditions. But, as explained in Chapter IV, diagnosing a food allergy presents problems, since laboratory tests are not particularly helpful.

Even when no allergy is apparent, children with eczema often have high levels of IgE, the allergy antibody. If you have a family history of eczema, you may be able to lower the risk of passing it on to your children by breast-feeding them as infants. There is also some evidence that withholding such potentially allergenic foods as milk, eggs and wheat during the first six months of life may protect infants with a family history of allergy and/or eczema from developing either condition. Discuss with your pediatrician the special nondairy infant formulas that are sometimes substituted for milk.

Treatment

If a food allergy is responsible for eczema, avoiding the food in question will bring the rash and itching under control. However, there are other measures you can take to lessen the discomfort.

- Take one or two twenty-minute baths per day in lukewarm water; pat the skin dry and lubricate with a moisturizer or nonirritating lotion. Acquafor, Acid Mantel or Vaseline are often recommended.
- Avoid rough, irritating clothing like wool and some synthetic fibers. Your best bet is cotton.
- Use unperfumed, nondeodorant soaps.

- Avoid sweating by keeping indoor temperature at 70 degrees.
- Keep children's nails well trimmed to prevent injury if they scratch; damage caused by scratching increases the risk of skin infection.

In addition to these self-help measures, your physician may recommend medication to control itching and treat the rash or any infections that develop. Antihistamines (Benadryl, Atarax or Periactin) taken orally can relieve itching. You may need antibiotics for skin infections, topical cortisone creams or ointments for the rash and, in severe cases, a course of oral steroid drugs when other forms of treatment don't work. See Chapter IX for a description of the drugs used to treat eczema.

Immunotherapy (see Chapter VIII) is not considered appropriate treatment for eczema, although it may be recommended for those who also have allergies to pollen.

ALLERGIC CONTACT DERMATITIS

This is a rash that develops as an allergic reaction to something that touches the skin. Poison ivy is the most common type of contact dermatitis: seven out of ten Americans are allergic to poison ivy and will develop an itchy rash if they come into contact with it. However, as with all other allergies, you have to be sensitized to poison ivy—you won't develop a rash the first time, but if you're among the unlucky allergic seven out of ten, you'll get one thereafter.

In addition to poison ivy, allergies to a long list of

plants, metals, chemicals, cosmetics and drugs can cause contact dermatitis. Symptoms are itching and a red rash on the area of skin that came into contact with the allergen. Blisters and swelling can also develop. Symptoms usually appear within twenty-four to forty-eight hours of exposure, but can be delayed for a week or more. Unlike eczema, a rash due to allergic contact dermatitis doesn't spread unless a wider area of skin comes into contact with the allergen. Contrary to common belief, fluid from a blister will *not* spread the rash to other parts of the body.

You can develop a rash from contact with a strong cleaning product or other chemical, but this type of dermatitis is due to irritation, not allergy.

Because so many substances can cause a contact allergy, it can be difficult to identify the one to blame. A careful medical history may narrow down the list, and a patch test (see Chapter VII) may confirm or rule out the suspected substance. Among the possibilities:

- Resin (not pollen) from ragweed, tumbleweed, pine trees, primrose, desert heliotrope, sagebrush, artichokes, chrysanthemums, daisies, tulips, tulip bulbs, poison oak, poison sumac and a wide variety of other plants.
- Ethylenediamine hydrochloride, an ingredient in antihistamines, antifungal creams and other medications
- p-Phenylenediamine, a chemical in hair dye, black, blue or brown clothing and fur dye
- Formalin and formaldehyde in cosmetics, insecticides and drip-dry and water-repellent fabrics
- Paraben, a chemical in some cosmetics

- Epoxy resin in glues, tapes and other adhesives
- Imidazolidinyl urea, a preservative in cosmetics
- Mercury in skin ointments and disinfectants
- Nickel in jewelry, coins, belt buckles, door handles
- Copper in coins, insecticides and fungicides

PREVENTION AND TREATMENT

Most symptoms will subside within a week or two, with or without treatment, as long as you don't come into contact with the allergen again. To avoid recurrences, observe the following precautions:

- Wear protective gloves or clothing whenever you anticipate exposure.
- Wash your clothes after exposure, since some allergens can cling.
- If you inadvertently touch the material you are allergic to, wash your skin immediately (within ten minutes if possible).
- You may be able to prevent contact between bare skin and certain plant allergens with a film of soap.

If a reaction does develop, you may get some relief by applying cool, wet compresses and a cortisone cream to the affected area. *Don't use antihistamine creams, lotions or ointments.* They contain ingredients capable of causing contact dermatitis and could make matters worse. Your doctor may prescribe oral or injected steroid drugs to control severe reactions. In general, the sooner this treatment begins, the more effective it will be. If you are taking oral steroids, be sure to follow dosage directions carefully; you probably won't have to take the drug for more than two weeks, but you will have to taper off the dosage slowly according to your doctor's directions to prevent side effects or a "rebound" flare-up of the dermatitis.

POISON IVY, OAK AND SUMAC

The culprit responsible for allergies to these three plants is an oily resin called *urushiol*. It can stick to clothing, gardening tools, outdoor gear, other plants and pets, and remains "active" and capable of triggering an allergic reaction for at least a year. Therefore, it is important to scrub your fingernails and clean any clothing, towels, sheets or other object (including pets) thoroughly. Otherwise, you risk reexposure each time you touch anything with urushiol on it. Smoke from burning poison-ivy plants can provoke skin reactions and may cause problems if inhaled.

The rash, bumps and blisters from contact with poison ivy, oak or sumac usually develop within hours of exposure, but can be delayed for as long as ten days. The itch and discomfort are most intense for the first five days after the rash develops; the reaction usually subsides within a week or two with or without treatment. Infections can occur as a result of scratching the rash. Bacteria from the hands and fingernails can easily penetrate skin, especially if blisters have broken. Symptoms of infection include fever and/or swollen glands.

A number of other plants of the same family can

cause contact dermatitis in those allergic to poison ivy, oak or sumac. These include cashew, mango, ginkgo, Japanese lacquer and Indian-marking nut trees.

If you come into contact with poison ivy, oak or sumac, wash your skin within five minutes to remove the urushiol. If you get it all off, you can prevent a reaction; unfortunately, washing won't help after five minutes has elapsed.

Treatment is the same as for the other forms of allergic contact dermatitis. (See previous section, p. 78.)

HIVES AND ANGIOEDEMA

The difference between hives and angioedema is that hives (known medically as *urticaria*) blossom on the surface of the skin while angioedema occurs in deeper layers of skin. Hives can be large or small, reddish or white, but whatever the size and color, they itch constantly and maddeningly.

Angioedema doesn't itch, but can be painful and even life-threatening if the swelling affects the tongue, throat or other part of the breathing apparatus. It should not be confused with a nonallergic, inherited condition, *hereditary angioedema*. This rare and life-threatening condition is due to the absence of the enzyme C1-esterase inhibitor and can cause swelling in the face, arms, legs and airways. Treatment is available.

While both hives and angioedema can be triggered by allergy, in between 70 and 90 percent of all cases the cause is never identified. Ironically, chances for pinpointing the triggering factor are lowest among chronic cases that recur periodically. The most likely culprits are foods or drugs, but any of the following can be responsible:

- Insect stings
- Exposure to cold temperatures
- Stress
- Physical exercise
- Heat exposure
- Ultraviolet light (from sun or sunlamp)
- Pressure from tight clothing
- Pressure from gripping an object
- Pressure from being in the same position for a long time
- Pollen, dust or animal dander
- Pressure from drawing an implement across or writing on the skin.

Foods

Food allergies can cause hives. Recurrent or chronic cases are usually due to foods such as milk, eggs, wheat, that are eaten on a daily basis. Intermittent episodes are more likely to be due to seasonal foods or those that aren't ordinarily part of your diet. Sulfites used as preservatives can also be to blame and, in rare cases, hives are due to the food additive tartrazine, a coloring agent (see Chapter IV).

Drugs

Hives can be a reaction to any drug, but the ones most often associated with an outbreak are penicillin and aspirin. In addition, other antibiotics and a wide variety of medications, both prescription and nonprescription, have been associated with outbreaks of hives. Among them: drugs containing aspirin, some laxatives, barbiturates, insulin, sulfa drugs, tranquilizers, codeine and many others too numerous to list here.

Diagnosis and Treatment

Since the factor that triggers hives is seldom identified, a thorough medical history and careful record keeping are the only way to pinpoint the culprit. If a specific food is suspected, skin testing may reveal whether it is responsible. There are no other medical tests that can help except in the rare instance that hives are due to parasitic infection. (This is extremely rare and probably would be suspected only if you had been traveling in areas of the world where parasitic diseases are common.)

The best treatment for hives is prevention—avoiding the substances or situations likely to bring on an attack. Some doctors suggest avoiding aspirin and foods containing sulfites and tartrazine.

While there is no "cure" for hives and you may never know what causes yours, you can relieve the symptoms:

- Oral antihistamines can relieve the itch and may reduce swelling. They also can help prevent hives and angioedema. It may take some trial and error to find the one that works best for you. Among those most frequently recommended are hydroxyzine (Atarax, Vistaril), diphenhydramine (Benadryl) and cyproheptadine (Periactin). (See Chapter IX for more information on these drugs.)

- Corticosteroids may be prescribed for relief of severe cases. Follow the doctor's directions carefully and take the medication only in the dosage prescribed, for as long as directed. You will have to taper off use of these drugs to prevent a "rebound" recurrence of your hives.
- Epinephrine (Adrenalin) may be needed when severe angioedema affects breathing. If you are subject to these attacks, you may have to carry injectable epinephrine as a precaution. (See the section on Emergencies, page xlvii, for instructions.)

CHAPTER VII

TESTING

▼

I F you know what causes your symptoms, you may not need allergy testing. However, if you have a severe allergy or symptoms that may or may not stem from an allergy, testing can help identify the problem and, in some cases, point the way toward the most effective treatment.

Helpful as it can be, however, allergy testing is often inappropriate, and can lead to mistaken diagnosis and unnecessary treatment. In 1989 the American College of Physicians issued a position paper warning against overtesting and noting that some doctors unnecessarily test patients for up to three hundred different allergies. The doctors who prepared the statement maintain that it is rarely necessary to test for more than fifty allergens, and, if food allergy isn't suspected, testing for thirty is usually more than enough.

The American College of Allergy and Immunology, a professional organization representing physicians who specialize in allergy treatment, takes the position that skin testing for allergy is generally more reliable, more convenient and less expensive than blood tests.

Both groups warn that testing is appropriate only

when a patient's medical history is strongly suggestive of allergy.

SKIN TESTS

There are four different types.

Prick (Scratch) Test

METHOD: The skin is pricked or scratched with a needle and a drop of an extract of an allergen is placed on the scratch or prick mark; you can be tested for up to thirty different allergies at the same time; this will mean thirty separate pricks or scratches.

WHEN RECOMMENDED: For patients whose medical histories suggest allergy; usually the first test ordered when allergy is suspected.

PREPARATION: If taking antihistamines, you will have to stop them two to five days before the test, depending on the particular drug.

DISCOMFORT: Minimal; the scratch is superficial, not deep enough to cause bleeding.

RESULTS: If you are allergic to any of the substances, you will develop a swollen red welt at the scratch or prick; any welt less than five millimeters large may not be significant. It usually takes between ten and twenty minutes for the reaction to occur.

RELIABILITY: If you don't develop a reaction to a test allergen, you can be certain that you are *not* allergic to it. However, you can have a positive reaction to a substance that causes you no problems. If so, you can safely ignore results, although there is a chance that symptoms may show up later in life. This is considered the most sensitive and specific test for allergies to foods and pollens.

RISK: A very small risk of a systemic (anaphylactic) reaction. A doctor should be present and emergency equipment available.

Intradermal

METHOD: Injection below the skin of a small amount of diluted allergen extract; you can be tested for ten or more allergies at the same time.

WHEN RECOMMENDED: When scratch or prick tests are negative but patient history *strongly* suggests a particular allergen.

PREPARATION: Same as prick test, above.

DISCOMFORT: Mild and transitory.

RESULTS: Usually apparent within ten to twenty minutes; development of swelling, itching and a red welt larger than five millimeters indicates allergy.

RELIABILITY: Generally more sensitive than prick (scratch) test but less specific; *not* a reliable test for food allergies; using too high a concentration of allergen extract can falsely indicate allergy where none exists.

RISK: A small danger of a systemic (anaphylactic) reaction; this risk is slightly higher than for prick tests; a doctor should be present and emergency equipment available.

Titration

METHOD: Injection of stronger and stronger concentrations of a suspected allergen to find the amount capable of triggering a reaction.

WHEN RECOMMENDED: In preparation for starting immunotherapy (allergy shots, see Chapter VIII), usually to insect venom, or to determine the effectiveness of ongoing immunotherapy. This test is a follow-up when the allergen has already been identified; its use for more than two allergens suggests that it has been improperly recommended.

PREPARATION: Same as prick test, above.

DISCOMFORT: Minimal

RESULTS: A skin reaction indicative of allergy (swelling, itching, redness, a welt five millimeters or larger).

RELIABILITY: *Warning: Very high concentrations may produce a reaction even in the nonallergic; some doctors may inappropriately recommend immunotherapy on the basis of a reaction to a high concentration of test material.*

RISK: Same as prick test, above.

Patch Test

METHOD: Small patches of absorbent materials are soaked with an allergen extract and applied to the back or forearm; these are covered with a bandage and left in place for forty-eight hours.

WHEN RECOMMENDED: In cases of contact dermatitis (see Chapter VI) that may be due to allergy.

PREPARATION: Same as prick test, above.

DISCOMFORT: Itching or blistering may develop as a response to the test allergens.

RESULTS: A positive reaction includes itching, blistering, redness.

RELIABILITY: Effective method, especially for contact allergies to metals and chemicals.

RISK: None.

Blood Tests

Only one blood test, the Radioallergosorbent (RAST) test, is available for diagnosing allergy. It can measure amounts of IgE specific to a suspected allergen. For example, if you have hay fever, it can confirm that you have antibodies to ragweed pollen circulating in your blood.

METHOD: Blood is drawn and then mixed in test tubes with a number of allergens, which are then analyzed for the presence of allergen-specific IgE.

WHEN RECOMMENDED: When the risk of an anaphylactic reaction makes skin testing too dangerous; when severe and extensive eczema makes skin testing impractical; when symptoms are so severe that antihistamine cannot be discontinued to permit accurate skin testing.

DISCOMFORT: Minimal

RESULTS: Available in twenty-four hours.

RELIABILITY: Less sensitive and more expensive than skin testing.

RISK: None

PROVOCATION TESTS

Sometimes the only way to confirm an allergy is to deliberately provoke the symptoms it causes. These tests may also be used to convince a patient that an allergy is *not* responsible for symptoms.

Bronchial Provocation

METHOD: Patient inhales increasing concentrations of allergen suspected of causing asthma or hay-fever symptoms; the dose is increased until symptoms occur or until it becomes so high that it would irritate the airways of nonallergic patients.

WHEN RECOMMENDED: *Rarely;* used primarily in allergy research because it is expensive, time-consuming and uncomfortable; may be used when skin-test results are not specific or conclusive or when the tests themselves are considered inadequate.

RESULTS: When positive, brings on allergy symptoms.

DISCOMFORT: Although not painful, the procedure and the setting may be intimidating; patients may have to inhale via a nebulizer or enter a special exposure chamber; after each inhalation, measurements are taken of the amount of air that can be exhaled. Because symptoms may be delayed, *patients must be medically monitored for eight hours after the test.*

RISK: Small risk of severe asthmatic reaction; testing should be done only by an experienced physician in a facility equipped to handle emergencies.

Oral Provocation

METHOD: Eliminating foods suspected of causing allergic reaction; if symptoms disappear, foods are reintroduced one by one every few days to see if symptoms recur; to prevent a psychosomatic reaction from occurring, foods sometimes are reintroduced in capsule form so that the patient doesn't know which is which; in "single blinded" food challenges, the patient doesn't know which food is being reintroduced; in more reliable "double blinded" challenges, the doctor doesn't know either (someone uninvolved with the testing process keeps the records).

WHEN RECOMMENDED: When symptoms are not typical of allergy but may be due to intolerance; when food allergy has previously been diagnosed on the basis of inappropriate or invalid tests; when several skin-test results are positive to determine which food is to blame for symptoms.

PREPARATION: None

DISCOMFORT: Only that due to symptoms that may be provoked by reintroducing an allergenic food.

RESULTS: If allergy is present, symptoms will appear when the allergenic food is introduced; if not, allergy can be ruled out.

RELIABILITY: Extremely reliable; the "double blind challenge" is the "gold standard" of allergy testing.

RISK: Can bring on severe asthma attack or, in susceptible individuals, anaphylactic shock. *Should never be performed on anyone who has suffered anaphylactic shock due to food allergy;* requires expert and experienced medical supervision; should be performed only in a facility equipped to handle emergencies.

UNPROVEN TESTS

A number of questionable testing methods have been vigorously promoted and continue to be offered by some physicians despite the fact that they have not been proved reliable in the diagnosis of allergies:

CYTOTOXIC TESTING (BRYAN'S TEST): This blood test ostensibly diagnoses food or inhalant allergies by combining extracts of suspect foods or inhaled allergens with white blood cells taken from a small sample of the patient's blood. Theoretically, if an allergy exists, changes will occur in white cells in response to the allergen. Cytotoxic testing has been studied extensively and found ineffective. White cell samples from people with known food allergies have shown no changes at all when submitted for cytotoxic testing. And results of tests of the same blood samples have differed from day to day and laboratory to laboratory. Despite scientific findings that cytotoxic testing is worthless, it is still advertised and used.

SUBCUTANEOUS AND SUBLINGUAL PROVOCATION: *Subcutaneous* tests involve injection of allergen extracts under the skin; in sublingual testing, the allergen is placed under the tongue. If a low dose doesn't bring on a reaction, higher and higher doses are administered. Adherents of these tests consider them positive for allergy upon development of symptoms anywhere in the body. Headache, cough, nausea, depression and other mood states are considered indicative of allergy. As soon as the reaction occurs, additional doses of the allergen are administered to "neutralize" the reaction. There is no scientific evidence that this method works; any perceived reaction or improvement probably is due to the power of suggestion, not the procedure itself.

PULSE TEST: This unproved method identifies food allergy on the basis of an increased pulse rate after eating a particular food. Introduced fifty years ago, this test was abandoned as unreliable; it recently has been reintroduced, although there is no new evidence suggesting that it is worthwhile.

KINESIOLOGY TESTING: This involves tests of muscle strength after eating or sublingual provocation with a suspect food. Supposedly, muscle strength decreases in the presence of allergy. There is no medical evidence that this method has any merit.

ALLERGY SHOTS

▼

THE best treatment for allergy is avoiding whatever sets off your symptoms. If that's not possible, drugs usually can prevent reactions or relieve symptoms that can't be forestalled. When all else fails, some people can benefit from allergy shots or immunotherapy designed to eliminate *or reduce* symptoms by building tolerance for the allergen. Immunotherapy is effective only against certain types of allergies:

- Severe (anaphylactic) reactions to insect stings.
- Hay fever and some other seasonal allergies to pollen.
- Some cases of asthma due to allergies to pollen, dust mites or animal dander.

Food and drug allergies *cannot* be treated with immunotherapy, although occasionally allergy shots for drug allergies can provide temporary protection when the drug in question is the only available treatment for an illness (see Chapter IV). Immunotherapy is *never* appropriate for any of the following conditions:

- Chronic bronchitis
- Emphysema
- Nonallergic rhinitis or asthma

- Allergies or other disorders affecting the skin, gastrointestinal tract, nervous system.

Immunotherapy

Immunotherapy entails a major commitment. It may take months, even years, to see results. Treatment begins with injections of very small, diluted doses of the allergen. Each time a shot is given, a slightly higher dose is used, until reaching a maintenance level that does not provoke allergy symptoms. At first, shots are administered once or twice a week; after a few months, a shot is given every other week, then every three weeks and then once a month. Immunotherapy for insect-sting allergies may go on indefinitely but treatment for other allergies usually continues until symptoms disappear or at least diminish substantially and remain under control for fifteen to eighteen months. Then shots can be discontinued. It may take up to five years to reach this point. Sometimes the allergy disappears permanently, but there is a chance that it will recur. If so, another round of immunotherapy may be recommended.

Do You Need Allergy Shots?

The only people who absolutely need allergy shots are those who have had anaphylactic reactions to insect stings and who, because of their life-style, are likely to be stung again. Beyond that, immunotherapy should be considered only under the following circumstances:
- Your symptoms are definitely due to allergy.
- You cannot avoid the allergen.

- Drugs either don't relieve symptoms or cause intolerable side effects.
- You react to only a few allergens, and you know what they are.
- There are no personal or professional obstacles in maintaining the immunotherapy schedule your doctor recommends.
- You are not pregnant. (Sometimes immunotherapy for insect-sting allergy can be initiated during pregnancy.)
- You have no diseases and are taking no drugs that would increase the danger of an adverse reaction to an allergy shot.
- You do *not* have severe, poorly controlled asthma.

As a general rule, immunotherapy works better for children than for adults, but it isn't recommended for youngsters under the age of five. There are no guarantees that this type of treatment will control allergic symptoms or eliminate an allergy. Although it usually provides at least partial relief, it may be months before you see results, and even then you may have to continue taking antihistamines or other drugs.

Risks

Although immunotherapy is well-established and generally safe, there are some risks:
- It may not work or may provide only partial relief.
- Welts and swelling may develop at the injection site; these can last several hours, and in severe cases can persist for days. This type of local reaction is very common and usually doesn't mean you

have to discontinue immunotherapy. The reaction may disappear without treatment or an antihistamine may be recommended if symptoms are uncomfortable.

- Anaphylaxis can occur as a reaction to the injected allergen dose. While the risk is remote, it is real. *Immunotherapy should be administered only when a doctor is present and in a facility equipped to handle life-threatening emergencies.*
- Severe asthma attacks can develop. Here, too, the risk is small, although patients with asthma seem to be particularly susceptible to adverse reactions to allergy shots. Your doctor should have the staff and facilities to handle this emergency should it occur.

Because of the dangers involved, all patients should be observed in the doctor's office for at least thirty minutes following all allergy shots. Reactions tend to occur when high doses are administered, but can develop with low doses. Highly allergic patients may be started out on extremely low concentrations of the allergen. You may have to skip a dose if you have an infection or a worsening of your allergic symptoms, although sometimes a reduced dose can be administered.

CHAPTER IX

DRUGS

▼

ANY of the prescription as well as nonprescription drugs used to treat allergy can slow reaction time, impair judgment and reduce coordination as well as cause drowsiness. For this reason, you should not drive when taking these drugs.

ANTIHISTAMINES

These drugs combat symptoms by blocking the action of histamine, the body chemical released in response to an allergen.

Azatadine
PRESCRIPTION ONLY

BRAND NAMES: Optimine, Trinalin Repetabs
USUAL DOSE: 1–2 mg every twelve hours; dosage must be individualized by physician.
HOW TO TAKE: With food
MOST COMMON SIDE EFFECTS: Drowsiness, weakness,

blurred vision, dry nose, mouth and throat, impaired urination, stomach distress.

PRECAUTIONS: Don't take if you have asthma, bronchitis or pneumonia; drinking alcohol can magnify the drug's sedative effect; avoid if you have taken an MAO inhibitor for depression within the past two weeks.

Brompheniramine

Most of these drugs are available over the counter; some require a prescription.

BRAND NAMES: Dimetane, Dimetane Cough Syrup-DC, Dimetane DC, Dimetane Decongestant Elixir, Dimetane Decongestant Tablets, Dimetane DX, Dimetane Extentabs, Dimetane-Ten, Dimetapp Preparations, Disphrol, Drixoral Plus, Drixoral Syrup, Drixoral Tablets, Veltane.

USUAL DOSE: 4 mg every four to six hours or 8 to 12 mg of prolonged-action form every twelve hours; prescription drug dosage must be individualized by physician.

HOW TO TAKE: With food or milk.

MOST COMMON SIDE EFFECTS: Same as Azatadine, above.

PRECAUTIONS: Same as Azatadine, above.

Chlorpheniramine

Most of these drugs are available over the counter; some require a prescription; some are combined with a decongestant (see Phenylpropanolamine, p. 104).

BRAND NAMES: Alka-Seltzer Plus, Allerest Tablets,

Chlor-Trimeton, Contac Severe Cold Formula Caplets, Contac 12 Hour Capsules, CoTylenol Children's Liquid Cold Formula, CoTylenol Cold Caplets and Tablets, CoTylenol Liquid, CoTylenol Tablets, Deconamine, Demazin, Fedahist, Fedahist Expectorant, 4-Way Cold Tablets, Hycomine Compound, Isoclor, Naldecon, Novafed A, Ornade, Penntuss, Polaramine, Rynatan, Sine-Off Extra Strength Capsules, Sine-Off Tablets, Singlet, Sinutab Maximum Strength Capsules and Tablets, Sinutab Tablets, Sudafed Plus, Teldrin, Triaminic Allergy Tablets, Triaminic Chewable Tablets, Triaminic Cold Syrup and Tablets, Triaminicin.

USUAL DOSE: 4 milligrams every four to six hours or 8 to 23 milligrams (prolonged action) every twelve hours.

HOW TO TAKE: With food or milk; don't crush or chew prolonged-action tablets or capsules.

MOST COMMON SIDE EFFECTS: Same as Azatadine, above.

PRECAUTIONS: Same as Azatadine, above.

Clemastine
PRESCRIPTION ONLY

BRAND NAMES: Tavist, Tavist-D, Tavist-1.

USUAL DOSE: 1.34 mg twice daily or 2.68 mg three times daily; dosage must be individualized by physician.

HOW TO TAKE: With food or milk.

MOST COMMON SIDE EFFECTS: Same as Azatadine, above.

PRECAUTIONS: Same as Azatadine, above.

Diphenhydramine

Some of these drugs are available by prescription only; others are available over the counter.

BRAND NAMES: Ambenyl Syrup, Benadryl, Benylin, Compoz, Excedrin P.M., Nytol, Sleep-Eze, Sominex 2, Twilite, Valdrene.

USUAL DOSE: 25 to 50 mg every four to six hours.

HOW TO TAKE: With food or after eating.

MOST COMMON SIDE EFFECTS: Same as Azatadine, above, although drowsiness may occur more frequently and be more pronounced.

PRECAUTIONS: Same as Azatadine, above.

Hydroxyzine
PRESCRIPTION ONLY

BRAND NAMES: Marax, Marax DF

USUAL DOSE: 25 to 100 mg three to four times per day.

HOW TO TAKE: With or without food.

MOST COMMON SIDE EFFECTS: Same as Azatadine, above; also "hangover" effect if used to induce sleep.

PRECAUTIONS: Avoid if you are taking another sedative; can cause seizures in those with seizure disorders; alcohol can increase sedative effect.

Promethazine
PRESCRIPTION ONLY

BRAND NAMES: K-Phen, Pentazine, Phenergan, Phenergan D, Phenergan with Codeine, Prorex.

USUAL DOSE: 12.5 to 25 mg every four to six hours as needed; total daily dose not to exceed 150 mg.

HOW TO TAKE: With or following food.

MOST COMMON SIDE EFFECTS: Drowsiness, lethargy, impaired concentration, dry mouth, constipation, impaired urination; may affect tolerance for contact lenses.

PRECAUTIONS: Drinking alcohol can increase or accelerate drowsiness; drug can become less effective with long-term use.

Terfenadine
PRESCRIPTION ONLY

BRAND NAMES: Seldane, Seldane-D

USUAL DOSE: 60 mg every eight to twelve hours; total daily dosage not to exceed 360 mg.

HOW TO TAKE: With food or milk.

MOST COMMON SIDE EFFECTS: Dry nose, mouth, throat. *This drug is one of the few antihistamines that does not cause drowsiness.*

PRECAUTIONS: Avoid if you have bronchial asthma, bronchitis or pneunomia.

Triprolidine
NONPRESCRIPTION

BRAND NAMES: Actidil, Actifed, Actifed with Codeine.

USUAL DOSE: 2.5 mg every four to six hours.

HOW TO TAKE: With food or milk.

MOST COMMON SIDE EFFECTS: Same as Azatadine, above.

PRECAUTIONS: Same as Azatadine, above.

DECONGESTANTS

Most of these drugs are nonprescription products for the relief of nasal congestion. Some are available as eye drops to relieve itching, reddened and swollen eyes, symptoms that sometimes accompany allergic rhinitis. They work by shrinking swollen nasal tissues and enlarging openings to the sinuses. While highly effective, long-term use of nonprescription decongestants can lead to a "rebound" effect in which the drug ceases to work and symptoms return, worse than ever. For this reason, they should be used for no longer than a week.

Oxymetazoline
NONPRESCRIPTION

BRAND NAMES: Afrin, Allerest 12 Hour Nasal, Coricidin Nasal Mist, Dristan Long Lasting, Duramist Plus, Duration, 4-Way Long Acting Nasal Spray, Neo-Synephrine 12 Hour, Nostrilla, NTZ Long Acting Nasal, Ocuclear, Sinarest 12-Hour Nasal Spray, Sinex Long-Acting.

USUAL DOSE: Nose drops and sprays: two to three drops or sprays into each nostril twice a day; eye drops: one or two drops in affected eye every six to eight hours.

HOW TO TAKE: As directed on package.

MOST COMMON SIDE EFFECTS: Dry or irritated nose, nervousness, insomnia; eye drops can irritate eyes.

PRECAUTIONS: Don't exceed recommended dose and don't take for more than one week in order to avoid "rebound" effect in which original symptoms return in worsened form; ask pharmacist about possible adverse interactions with other over-the-counter allergy or cold medications.

Phenylephrine

Most of these drugs are available over the counter, but some require a prescription; some are combined with an antihistamine. (See Brompheniramine, p. 98).

BRAND NAMES: Alconefrin, Dimetane Decongestant Elixir, Dimetane Expectorant-C, Dimetane Extentabs, Dimetapp, Dimetapp-A Preparations, Dimetapp-C, Dimetapp-DM, Dimetapp Infant Drops, Dimetapp with Codeine, Duo-Medihaler, Entex, Entex Liquid, 4-Way Nasal Spray, Hycomine Compound, Naldecon, Neo-Synephrine, Nostil, Rynatan, Sinex, Singlet.

USUAL DOSE: Nose drops or sprays: two or three drops into each nostril every four hours as needed; eye drops: one or two drops in affected eye every four to six hours; some of these drugs are available only by prescription; if you are taking one, follow your doctor's dosage instructions.

HOW TO TAKE: Tablets should be taken with food; prolonged-action tablets or capsules should not be crushed.

MOST COMMON SIDE EFFECTS: Dry, irritated nose, nervousness, insomnia.

PRECAUTIONS: See Oxymetazoline, above.

Phenylpropanolamine

Most of these drugs are available over the counter, but some require a prescription; some are combined with an antihistamine. (See Brompheniramine, page 98; Chlorpheniramine, page 98.)

BRAND NAMES: Alka-Seltzer Plus, Allerest, Contac Severe Cold Formula Tablets, Contac 12 Hour Capsules, Demazin, Dimetane Cough Syrup-DC, Dimetane Expectorant, Dimetane Expectorant-C, Dimetane Extentabs, Dimetapp, Entex, Entex LA, Entex Liquid, 4-Way Cold Tablets, Hycomine Pediatric Syrup, Hycomine Syrup, Naldecon, Naldecon-CX, Ornade, Ornex, Sine-Aid, Sine-Off Extra Strength Capsules, Sine-Off Tablets, Sinubid, Tavist-D, Triaminic Allergy Tablets, Triaminic Chewable Tablets, Triaminic Cold Syrup and Tablets, Triaminic DM, Triaminic Expectorant, Triaminic Expectorant with Codeine, Triaminic Expectorant DH, Triaminicin, Tuss-Ornade Liquid, Tuss-Ornade Spansules

USUAL DOSE: 12.5 to 37.5 mg every four to six hours as needed.

HOW TO TAKE: With or without food; don't crush prolonged-action tablets or capsules.

MOST COMMON SIDE EFFECTS: Nervousness, insomnia; can increase blood pressure in those susceptible; stomach irritation.

PRECAUTIONS: Consult doctor about excessive nervousness, restlessness, insomnia; this drug can dangerously overstimulate some people; ask pharmacist about other over-the-counter medications that can interact adversely with these products.

Pseudoephedrine

Most of these drugs are available over the counter, but some require a prescription; some are combined with an antihistamine. (See Brompheniramine, page 98; Chlorpheniramine, page 98).

BRAND NAMES: Actifed, Actifed with Codeine (prescription), Afrinol Repetabs, Cenafed, CoTylenol Children's Liquid Cold Formula, CoTylenol Tablets, Deconamine, Dimacol, Dimacol Liquid, Dimetane-DX, Disophrol, Drixoral Plus, Drixoral Syrup, Drixoral Tablets, Fedahist, Fedahist Expectorant, Fedrazil, Isoclor, Isoclor Expectorant, Novafed, Novafed A Capsules, Novahistex Cold Capsules, Phenergan-D, Seldane-D, Sine-Off Extra Strength Capsules, Sinutab Maximum Strength Capsules and Tablets, Sinutab Tablets, Sudafed, Sudafed Cough Syrup, Sudafed Plus, Sudafed 12 Hour, Trinalin Repetabs, Tussend, Tussend Expectorant.

USUAL DOSE: 30 to 60 mg every four to six hours; 120 mg (prolonged action) every eight to twelve hours or as directed by physician.

HOW TO TAKE: With or without food; do not crush capsules; do not exceed recommended dose.

MOST COMMON SIDE EFFECTS: Nervousness, insomnia.

PRECAUTIONS: To avoid insomnia, don't take within six hours of bedtime; caffeine in coffee, tea or cola drinks may worsen nervousness and/or insomnia due to drug use.

STEROIDS

These are powerful drugs used to treat severe asthma and symptoms of allergic rhinitis or allergic skin conditions that don't respond to less potent medications. No one knows precisely how steroids work, but they do reduce inflammation, which may play a role in asthma and allergy symptoms. With long-term use these drugs can lead to a number of serious side effects including mental or emotional disturbances, peptic ulcers, bone loss, cataracts, glaucoma, high blood pressure and high blood sugar.

Beclomethasone
PRESCRIPTION ONLY

BRAND NAMES: Beclovent, Beconase AQ Nasal Spray, Beconase Nasal Inhaler, Vancenase Nasal Inhaler, Vanceril

USUAL DOSE: Nasal inhaler (for allergic rhinitis): one inhalation two to four times per day; oral inhaler (for asthma control): two inhalations three to four times daily; severe asthma may require up to sixteen inhalations per day.

HOW TO TAKE: As needed

MOST COMMON SIDE EFFECTS: Fungus infections of mouth and throat (for oral inhaler).

PRECAUTIONS: Asthmatics should carry identification noting use of this drug.

Dexamethasone
PRESCRIPTION ONLY

BRAND NAMES: Decaderm, Decadron, Decadron-LA, Decadron Phosphate Ophthalmic, Decadron Phosphate Respihaler, Decadron Phosphate Turbinaire, Decadron with Xylocaine, Decaspray, Dexasone, Dexone, Hexadrol, Maxidex.

USUAL DOSE: Must be individualized by physician.

HOW TO TAKE: Some of the products listed above are nasal inhalers, some are creams, eye ointments, gels, injections, oral solutions and tablets; use inhalers, creams, ointments as per physician's instructions; take tablets with food or after eating.

MOST COMMON SIDE EFFECTS: Increased appetite, weight gain, water retention, increased susceptibility to infection, potassium loss.

PRECAUTIONS: Carry an identification card noting that you are using this drug; don't stop using it abruptly.

Methylprednisolone
PRESCRIPTION ONLY

BRAND NAMES: Medrol, Medrol Enpak.

USUAL DOSE: Must be individualized by physician.

HOW TO TAKE: Comes in ointment form, as a retention enema and as tablets. Take tablets with food or after eating.

MOST COMMON SIDE EFFECTS: Same as dexamethasone, above.

PRECAUTIONS: Same as dexamethasone, above.

Prednisolone
PRESCRIPTION ONLY

BRAND NAMES: Delta-Cortef, Prelone.
USUAL DOSE: Must be individualized by physician.
HOW TO TAKE: With food or after eating.
MOST COMMON SIDE EFFECTS: Same as dexamethasone, above.
PRECAUTIONS: Same as dexamethasone, above.

Prednisone
PRESCRIPTION ONLY

BRAND NAMES: Deltasone, Meticorten, Orasone.
USUAL DOSE: Must be individualized by physician.
HOW TO TAKE: With food or after eating.
MOST COMMON SIDE EFFECTS: Same as dexamethasone, above.
PRECAUTIONS: Same as dexamethasone, above.

Cromolyn
(Also known as Cromolyn sodium, sodium cromoglycate)
PRESCRIPTION ONLY

A relatively new drug for prevention of both asthma symptoms and the stuffy nose, itchy, tearing eyes and other symptoms of allergic rhinitis. It is effective in about 75 percent of all cases.

BRAND NAMES: Intal, Nasalcrom, Opticrom.
USUAL DOSE: Comes as eye drops, inhaler, inhalation powder, inhalation solution, nasal insufflator, nasal solution. Eye drops: one drop four to six times daily; in-

halation aerosol, two inhalations per day; inhalation powder, one capsule four times per day; inhalation solution, same as powder; nasal insufflator, at first 10 mg in each nostril every four to six hours; eventually every eight to twelve hours.

HOW TO TAKE: Nasal products must be inhaled.

MOST COMMON SIDE EFFECTS: Throat irritation, hoarseness, cough.

PRECAUTIONS: Do not use to reverse an acute asthma attack.

XANTHINES

These drugs block enzymes involved in the muscle constriction that characterizes asthmatic bronchial spasms. They may be used alone or in combination with other drugs to treat asthma.

Theophylline
PRESCRIPTION ONLY

BRAND NAMES: Accurbron, Amesec, Brondecon, Bronkaid Tablets, Bronkodyl, Bronkolixir, Bronkotabs, Choledyl, Constant-T, Elixicon, Elixophyllin, LāBID, Lodrane, Marax, Marax DF, Mudrane GG Elixir and Tablets, Mudrane Tablets, Quadrinal, Quibron, Quibron Plus, Quibron-T Dividose, Respbid, Slo-bid, Slo-Phyllin, Slo-Phyllin GG, Slo-Phyllin Gyrocaps, Somophyllin-CRT, Somophyllin-DF, Somophyllin-T, Sustaire.

USUAL DOSE: Comes as capsules, prolonged-action

capsules, elixir, oral solution, oral suspension, syrup, tablets, prolonged-action tablets. Dosage must be determined according to body weight; physician must individualize dose.

HOW TO TAKE: With food or after eating.

MOST COMMON SIDE EFFECTS: Nervousness, insomnia, rapid heart rate, increased urine volume.

PRECAUTIONS: Don't combine this drug with other medication for asthma unless instructed by your doctor.

BETA-ADRENERGIC BRONCHODILATORS

These powerful drugs for asthma relax bronchial muscle spasms.

Albuterol
PRESCRIPTION ONLY

BRAND NAMES: Proventil Inhaler, Proventil Tablets, Ventolin Inhaler, Ventolin Tablets, Rotacaps spin inhaler, Repetabs, long acting.

USUAL DOSE: Dosage must be individualized by physician.

HOW TO TAKE: Tablets can be taken with or without food; do not overuse inhalers.

MOST COMMON SIDE EFFECTS: Inhalers may dry and irritate mouth or throat and affect taste; tablets can cause nervousness and palpitations.

PRECAUTIONS: Ask doctor about interactions and possible toxicity when used in combination with other drugs for asthma; effectiveness may diminish with long-term use; prolonged use may affect heart rhythm.

Metaproterenol

BRAND NAMES: Alupent, Metaprel

USUAL DOSE: Must be individualized by physician.

HOW TO TAKE: With or without food; inhaled forms as per physician instructions.

MOST COMMON SIDE EFFECTS: Same as Albuterol, above.

PRECAUTIONS: Same as Albuterol, above; also, don't use within four hours of epinephrine; don't increase dosage without physician approval.

Terbutaline

BRAND NAMES: Brethaire, Brethine, Bricanyl.

USUAL DOSE: Must be individualized by physician.

HOW TO TAKE: Comes in tablet, injection and aerosol form; take tablets with or without food; do not overuse aerosol.

MOST COMMON SIDE EFFECTS: Same as Albuterol, above.

PRECAUTIONS: Ask doctor about interactions and possible toxicity when used in combination with other drugs for asthma; effectiveness may diminish with long-term use; prolonged use may affect heart rhythm. More-over, don't use within four hours of epinephrine; don't increase dosage without physician approval.

Epinephrine

Some of these drugs are available by prescription only; others can be purchased over the counter.

Also known as Adrenalin, epinephrine combats severe asthma attacks and is used to treat anaphylaxis, life-threatening allergic reactions. It relaxes constricted bronchial tubes, relieves nasal congestion, raises blood pressure and inhibits histamine release.

BRAND NAMES: Adrenalin, Bronkaid Mist, Epifrin, E-Pilo Preparations, Epitrate, Medihaler-Epi Preparations, Primatene Mist, Sus-Phrine, Vaponefrin, Epi-Pen, Ana-Kit (injectible epinephrine to treat anaphylaxis; see anaphylaxis on page xlvii).

USUAL DOSE: Must be individualized by physician.

HOW TO TAKE: Comes as aerosol, nose drops, solution for nebulizer and in injection form; wait a minute or two after inhaling before using again; get medical help if drug does not relieve symptoms within twenty minutes. Injected epinephrine is used to reverse anaphylaxis and severe asthmatic wheezing.

MOST COMMON SIDE EFFECTS: Nervousness, restlessness, anxiety, headache, palpitation, cold hands and feet, dry mouth and throat, tremor.

PRECAUTIONS: Do *not* use epinephrine except on the advice of your physician; avoid excessive use—too much can be fatal; discard if discolored or cloudy; follow doctor's instructions if combining epinephrine with any other drug for asthma treatment.

RESOURCES

▼

American Academy of Allergy and Immunology
611 East Wells Street
Milwaukee, WI 53202
(414) 272-6071

Patient-education materials on allergies and allergy treatment.

Asthma and Allergy Foundation of America
1717 Massachusetts Ave., NW
Washington, DC 20036
(800) 7-ASTHMA

Patient information materials on allergies; answers questions from the public on allergy testing, treatment and research; assists people in starting new support groups or maintaining existing groups. For support-group services contact:

Nancy Sanker, OTR
1412 Miramont Drive
Fort Collins, CO 80524
(303) 221-9165

National Institute of Allergy and Infectious Diseases
Office of Research Reporting and Public Response
9000 Rockville Pike
Bethesda, MD 20205
(301) 496-5717

Patient education materials, conducts and supports scientific research on the causes, prevention and treatment of allergies and other immune-system diseases.

American Lung Association
1740 Broadway
New York, NY 10019
(212) 245-8000

Educational materials about asthma and other respiratory diseases; maintains listing of camps for children with asthma. There are state and/or local chapters throughout the United States.

American Camping Association
Bradford Woods
Martinsville, Indiana 46151
(800) 428-CAMP

Maintains guide to accredited children's camps throughout the United States, including those for children with asthma.

National Jewish Center for Immunology and
    Respiratory Medicine
1400 Jackson Street
Denver, CO 80206
(800) 222-LUNG
In Colorado (800) 355-LUNG

Free telephone hot line for information on asthma and
food allergies as well as other respiratory disorders;
newsletters and patient-education materials.

ABLEDATA
Adaptive Equipment Center
Newington Children's Hospital
181 East Cedar Street
Newington, CT 06111
(800) 344-5405
In Connecticut: (203) 667-5405

Computer searches of products for the disabled, including air-filtering devices or breathing aids; searches up to
eight pages of information free. There is a charge for
further information.

American College of Allergy and Immunology
800 E. NW Highway, Suite 1080
Palatine, IL 60067
(708) 359-2800

Physician and patient-education materials on allergy
and asthma; physician referral service.

Mothers of Asthmatics
10875 Main Street, Suite 210
Fairfax, VA 22030
(703) 385-4403

Pamphlets and newsletter for parents of children with asthma.

Parents of Asthmatic/Allergic Children, Inc.
1407 Glen Haven Drive
Fort Collins, CO 80526
(303) 225-0227

Quarterly newsletter relating to asthma and allergy information and support services.

Eczema Association
1221 SW Yanhill
Suite 303
Portland, OR 97205
(503) 228-4430

Newsletter and brochures on eczema.

Peak Flow Meter Sources:

Mini-Wright Peak Flow Meter
Dura Pharmaceutical
P.O. Box 2209
Ramona, CA 92065
(800) 231-3195

Allergy Supply Company
P.O. Box 419
Fairfax Station, VA 22039
(800) 323-6744

ALLERGY AND ASTHMA RESEARCH CENTERS

The National Institute of Allergy and Infectious Diseases supports asthma and allergy research at the institutions listed below. All provide treatment, education or referrals.

- Brigham and Women's Hospital
  Boston, MA
- Duke University Medical Center
  Durham, NC
- Mayo Clinic
  Rochester, MN
- Northwestern University Medical School
  Chicago, IL
- Tufts University School of Medicine
  Boston, MA
- Scripps Clinic and Research Foundation
  LaJolla, CA
- State University of New York at Stony Brook
  Stony Brook, NY
- University of California, San Diego, Medical Center
  San Diego, CA
- University of Iowa Hospitals
  Iowa City, IA
- University of Texas, Dallas Health Science Center
  Dallas, TX
- University of Wisconsin Medical School
  Madison, WI

- Georgetown University School of Medicine
  Washington, DC
- Harvard Medical School, Children's Hospital
  Cambridge, MA
- Johns Hopkins University School of Medicine
  Baltimore, MD
- University of Alabama at Birmingham
  Birmingham, AL
- University of California at Los Angeles, School of Medicine
  Los Angeles, CA
- Washington University School of Medicine
  St. Louis, MO

FOODS AND BEVERAGES CONTAINING SULFITES

▼

N checking labels for sulfites,* look for the words *sulfur dioxide, sodium* and *potassium metabisulfite, sodium* and *potassium bisulfite,* and *sodium sulfite.*

- Canned mushrooms
- Canned and dried soups
- Dried salad-dressing mixes
- Frozen, canned or dried fruits and vegetables
- Potato chips
- Frozen French-fried potatoes

* The U.S. Food and Drug Administration bans use of sulfiting agents to prevent browning of unlabeled foods, including salad greens, peeled fruits, fresh potatoes and guacamole. All foods containing sulfite levels above ten parts per million must be labeled accordingly. Wines containing sulfites must be labeled.

- Pickles
- Sauerkraut
- Packaged sauce and gravy mixes
- Gelatin
- Dried fish
- Fresh shellfish (particularly shrimp)
- Frozen, canned or dried shellfish
- Wine vinegar
- Frozen doughs and other baked goods
- Fruit juices
- Wine
- Beer
- Cider
- Cordials

DRUGS
CONTAINING
ASPIRIN

▼

ANY over-the-counter drug containing the word *salicylate* in the active-ingredient list contains aspirin. These can include the following:

- Pain medications
- Cold tablets
- Drugs for stomach distress
- Some antihistamines
- Medications for menstrual distress
- Suntan lotions

The following prescription drugs:

- Darvon (pain killer)
- Fiorinal (for tension headaches)
- Percodan (painkiller)

ELIMINATION
DIETS

▼

IDENTIFYING a food allergy usually requires eliminating the suspected food or foods to see if symptoms disappear and then reintroducing them one by
one to see if symptoms recur.

EGG-FREE DIET

*Eggs must not be eaten in any form. No foods contain-
ing even small amounts of egg among the ingredients
can be eaten.*

Read labels carefully. Do not eat if egg, egg white,
dried egg or albumin are among the ingredients. The
foods listed below usually are made with eggs and
should not be eaten on this diet unless you can ascertain
from the label that no eggs in any form have been used
in their preparation:

• Cakes and cookies unless baked at home with egg-
free recipes (substitute one-half teaspoon baking

powder for each egg; commercially available *replacement—not* substitute—eggs are permitted. Substitutes usually eliminate only yolks; egg replacements contain no egg.)
- Chocolates, marshmallows, fondants
- Soups containing egg noodles (includes alphabet); any other soup made with eggs
- Mayonnaise
- Custards, puddings, ice cream, filing for cream pies, including coconut, lemon and pumpkin pies
- Eggnog, egg creams
- French toast
- Fritters
- Pancakes (eggless pancake mixes are commercially available)
- Muffins, rolls, bagels, doughnuts and any breads containing eggs (most bread does *not* contain eggs, but check the ingredients listed on packaged breads and ask when buying freshly baked bread)
- Meat loaf and other meat, chicken or fish dishes made with egg or dipped in batter containing eggs
- Meringues
- Pretzels
- Egg substitutes
- Sauces and salad dressing containing eggs; these include hollandaise sauce, dressing for Caesar salad, Russian dressing and any dressings that include mayonnaise.

MILK-FREE DIET

Milk in any form may *not* be eaten. You must eliminate all foods in which milk is an ingredient.

Read labels carefully. The following words indicate that milk or milk products are present: milk, whey, dried milk solids, casein, lactalbumin, sodium caseinate, potassium caseinate, calcium caseinate, butter, cheese, margarine, curds. Do not assume that a product once milk-free will remain so. Check ingredients continually to be sure. The following foods may *not* be eaten:

- Milk
- Cream
- Yogurt
- Lact-aid
- Acidophilus milk
- Ice cream and ice milk, sherbets made with milk, frozen yogurt
- Cream sauces and soups, white sauces
- Butter
- Cheese
- Margarine (except parve)
- Baked goods (including breads) made with milk; check labels
- Vegetables (such as mashed potatoes) prepared with milk, cheese, butter or cream
- Instant cocoa, breakfast mixes and other products containing dried milk
- Cereals containing milk (check *all* labels)

WHEAT-FREE DIET

You may *not* eat wheat in any form. Check labels carefully to be sure that even small amounts are not among food ingredients. The following words indicate that wheat in some form is present: *wheat, flour, wheat germ, wheat starch, bran, modified food starch, graham flour, farina, semolina.*

The following foods may *not* be eaten:
- Breads, crackers and other baked goods (except those made without wheat; be careful, rye bread and cornbread usually contain wheat)
- Cereal (unless you ascertain that wheat is *not* an ingredient)
- All forms of pasta and noodles made from wheat
- Fried chicken and other fried foods that have been rolled in bread crumbs or flour made from wheat
- Meat loaf and other foods containing bread crumbs, cracker crumbs, cereal or other forms of wheat. This includes sausages, hot dogs and some cold cuts.
- Sauces and gravies thickened with flour
- Prepared salad dressings thickened with flour or other forms of wheat
- Pancakes, waffles and fritters
- Any other food containing wheat in any form.

SOY-FREE DIET

Soybeans in any form *cannot* be eaten. Many processed foods contain soy in various forms. Check all labels carefully to be sure that no soy or soybeans are present. The following words indicate that soybeans are among the ingredients: soybean, soy flour, soy protein, soy protein isolate, soy sauce, soya, tamari, vegetable protein (unless the vegetable is specified and is *not* soybeans), vegetable broth (unless the vegetable is specified and is *not* soybeans), cereal. However, since the allergenic protein has been removed from the following foods, you may continue to eat them: soy oil/soybean oil; lecithin/soy lecithin.

FOOD FAMILIES

▼

I N rare instances, people with food allergies may develop reactions to closely related foods. Here is a list of food families. An asterisk (*) marks those families with surprising members.

- Anise, caraway seed, carrot, celery, celery seed, coriander, cumin, dill, fennel, parsley, parsnip
- Apple, pear, quince
- Artichoke, chicory, dandelion, endive, escarole, lettuce, sunflower seeds, tarragon
- Asparagus, chives, garlic, leeks, onion, sarsaparilla
- Avocado, bay leaves, cinnamon, sassafras
- Banana, plantain
- Barley, corn, millet, oats, rice, rye, sorghum
- Beet, spinach, Swiss chard
- *Black-eyed peas, licorice, lima beans, navy beans, peanuts, peas, pinto beans, string beans, tragacanth (a green)
- Blueberries, currants, gooseberries, mulberries
- Blackberries, boysenberries, loganberries, raspberries, strawberries
- Buckwheat, rhubarb, sorrel
- Cabbage, broccoli, brussel sprouts, cauliflower,

collards, horseradish, kale, mustard, radish, ruta-
baga, turnip, watercress
- Cantaloupe, casaba melon, cucumber, honeydew
melon, Persian melon, pumpkin, squash, water-
melon
- Cashews, mango, pistachios
- Chocolate, cocoa, cola
- Coconut, dates
- Grapefruit, kumquat, lemon, lime, oranges, tanger-
ines
- Ginger, cardamom, tumeric
- Mint, basil, peppermint, rosemary, sage, spearmint
- *Peaches, plums, cherries, almonds, apricots
- Pecans, walnuts, butternuts, hickory nuts
- *Peppers: bell peppers, cayenne peppers, chili pep-
pers; eggplant, paprika, potatoes, tomatoes
- Fowl: chicken, duck, goose, pheasant, guinea hen,
quail, squab, turkey, eggs
- Crustaceans: crabs, crayfish, lobster, shrimp; squid
- Mollusks: abalone, clams, mussels, oysters, scal-
lops
- Fish: all freshwater and saltwater fish
- Meat: beef, goat, horse, pork, lamb; milk from
these animals
- Turtle, rattlesnake

GLOSSARY

Most of the following terms are used in this book or may be used by a physician in discussing allergy. Some popularly used but medically outdated terminology is included.

ACIDOPHILUS—Fermented milk used to change bacterial content of intestine; tolerated better than milk by the lactose intolerant. See Lactose intolerance.

ADRENOCORTICOIDS—See corticosteroids.

AIRWAY OBSTRUCTION—Blockage or narrowing of tubes that carry air to lungs; occurs in asthma.

ALBUMIN—Protein in egg whites; highly allergenic.

ALLERGEN—Substance responsible for allergic reaction.

ALLERGENIC EXTRACT—Substance used to test for allergy; made from an allergen such as dustmites and added to a fluid.

ALLERGIC BRONCHOPULMONARY ASPERGILLOSIS—Disease that occurs among allergic asthmatics due to fungus in lungs.

ALLERGIC CONTACT DERMATITIS—See Contact dermatitis

ALLERGIC REACTION—Immune-system response to allergen.

ALLERGIC RHINITIS—Inflammation of nasal membranes caused by allergy to pollen and other allergens.

ALLERGIC SHINERS—Dark circles under the eyes of some allergic children due to swelling and impaired blood flow.

ALLERGIC TENSION-FATIGUE SYNDROME—Group of symptoms including irritability, anxiety and fatigue seen in some children with food allergies.

ALLERGIST—Physician specializing in allergy treatment.

ALLERGY—Immune-system response to ordinarily harmless substances among susceptible individuals.

ANAPHYLAXIS—Severe, potentially life-threatening allergic reaction.

ANAPHYLACTOID—Reaction similar to anaphylaxis (see above) not caused by IgE antibody.

ANGIOEDEMA—Anaphylactic reaction characterized by swelling of the skin and underlying tissues.

ANTIBODY—Protein produced by immune system in response to foreign substance in the body.

ANTIGEN—Substance triggering immune-system response.

ANTIHISTAMINE—Drug used to treat allergy symptoms due to histamine, a body chemical released during allergic reaction.

ASTHMA—Breathing disorder sometimes caused by allergy.

ATOPIC—Allergic.

ATOPIC DERMATITIS—Eczema; skin inflammation sometimes caused by allergy.

ALVEOLI—Tiny air sacs in lungs.

B CELLS—See B lymphocytes.

B LYMPHOCYTES—White blood cells in immune system; involved in antibody production.

BAGASSOSIS—Occupational lung disease caused by allergic reaction to moldy sugar cane.

BASOPHIL—White blood cell similar to mast cell; see mast cells.

BRADYKININ—Body chemical involved in allergic reactions; contracts smooth muscle, stimulates mucus secretion.

BRONCHIAL TREE—Tubes and air sacs that supply air to lungs.

BRONCHIOLE—Tiny airway; part of bronchial tree.

BRONCHOCONSTRICTION—Tightening of muscles surrounding airways to lungs.

BRONCHODILATOR—Drug to treat asthma; relaxes constricted airways that obstruct breathing.

BRONCHOSPASM—Constriction of muscles surrounding bronchial tubes.

CANDIDA ALBICANS—Yeast that can cause infection; unproved allergy theory holds that *Candida* causes wide variety of symptoms; also called *Monilia*.

CELIAC DISEASE—Intestinal disorder caused by intolerance of gluten, a constituent of wheat and other grains.

CHALLENGE TEST—Medical test to diagnose allergy to certain substances; involves exposure to small amounts of suspected allergen; also called Provocation test.

CLINICAL ECOLOGY—Unproved medical theory that allergies to foods, synthetic materials, chemicals and environmental pollutants underlie chronic fatigue and a wide variety of common symptoms for which no other physical cause can be found.

CLOXACILLIN ALLERGY—Allergy to cloxacillin, an antibiotic related to penicillin.

COLD URTICARIA—Hives caused by exposure to cold temperatures.

COMPLEMENT SYSTEM—Proteins involved in immune-system responses to foreign substances.

CONJUNCTIVA—Outer membrane of eyes; can become irritated or inflamed as a result of nasal allergy.

CORTICOSTEROIDS—Powerful drugs used to treat inflammation and swelling due to allergic reactions; may be referred to as steroids or adrenocorticoids.

CROHN'S DISEASE—Chronic gastrointestinal disorder; may predispose to food allergy.

CROMOLYN SODIUM—Drug for asthma and hay fever.

CROSS REACTION—Reaction to foods closely related to allergen.

CYANOSIS—Lack of oxygen; lips and fingernail beds turn blue; sign of impending suffocation during asthma attack; requires emergency treatment.

CYTOTOXIC TESTING—Unproved test for food allergies; considered unreliable.

DANDER—Tiny particles of animal skin; common allergen.

DECONGESTANTS—Nasal sprays or nose drops for relief of nasal congestion due to allergies, colds.

DESENSITIZATION—See Immunotherapy.

DUST MITES—Microorganisms found in household dust; common allergen.

ECZEMA—Skin condition often due to allergy; skin becomes red, dry and itchy; see Atopic dermatitis.

EDEMA—Swelling.

ELIMINATION DIET—Method of identifying food responsible for allergy by removing it and then returning it to diet.

EOSINOPHILS—White blood cells involved in allergic reactions.

EPINEPHRINE—Adrenaline; used to treat anaphylaxis.

ERYTHEMA—Reddened area of skin.

ERYTHEMA MULTIFORME—Severe, potentially life-threatening type of hives; usually due to allergy to sulfa drugs.

EUSTACHIAN TUBES—Tubes in back of throat; one leads to each ear.

EXTRACT—See Allergenic extract.

FARMER'S LUNG—Allergy to moldy hay; found among farmers.

FAVISM—Sensitivity to fava beans.

FOOD ALLERGY—Reaction to certain foods; symptoms typically affect the digestive tract.

FUNGUS—Primitive organisms, including molds, which are common allergens.

GLUTEN—Constituent of wheat and other grains; gluten intolerance is called Celiac disease.

GLYCOPROTEINS—Food components most likely to trigger food allergy.

HAY FEVER—Allergy to grass pollens; see Allergic rhinitis.

HEREDITARY ANGIOEDEMA—Rare inherited disease causing painful swelling of face, larynx, airways, intestines, arms and legs; can be fatal if air supply is cut off by swelling.

HISTAMINE—Chemical released by mast cells during allergic reaction; triggers typical allergy symptoms. See Mast cells.

HUFFER—Medical slang for peak-flow meter; see Peak-flow meter.

HYMENOPTERA—Order of insects responsible for most allergic sting reactions. Includes bees, hornets, wasps, yellow jackets.

HYPERSENSITIVITY—Condition that results from formation of IgE antibody to allergen; will result in allergic reaction upon reexposure.

HYPERSENSITIVITY PNEUMONITIS—Lung disorders due to allergy to dust and other inhaled allergens.

HYPOSENSITIZATION—Term once used for allergy treatment; see Immunotherapy.

HYPOTENSION—Low blood pressure.

IMMUNE SYSTEM—Body's defense mechanism; cells and chemicals that protect against disease.

IMMUNOGLOBULINS—Body proteins, including antibodies.

IMMUNOGLOBULIN A (IgA)—Antibodies found in saliva, tears and other body fluids; first line of defense against infection.

IMMUNOGLOBULIN E (IgE)—Antibody responsible for allergies.

IMMUNOGLOBULIN G (IgG)—Antibody produced in response to infection and other health threats.

IMMUNOGLOBULIN M (IgM)—Antibodies that protect against bacteria.

IMMUNOTHERAPY—Allergy treatment involving injection with small amounts of allergen; previously called desensitization, hyposensitization; also called allergy shots.

INFLAMMATION—Swelling, pain and redness due to injury; can be internal or external.

INHALER—Device used to administer some drugs for asthma; delivers metered dose via mouth.

INTRADERMAL TEST—Allergy skin test requiring injection of allergen into skin.

INTRINSIC ASTHMA—Term once used for nonallergic asthma.

LACTOSE INTOLERANCE—Inability to digest dairy products due to absence of enzyme lactase.

LEGUMES—Vegetables including soybeans and peanuts; common food allergens.

LYMPHOCYTE—White blood cell involved in immune responses.

MAST CELLS—Cells sensitized when allergy is present; release histamine to set in motion allergy symptoms.

MEDIATORS—Immune-system substances that activate physical response to antigens; histamine is best-known mediator; contained in mast cells.

METERED-DOSE INHALER (MDI)—Portable nebulizer for administration of inhaled drugs for asthma and allergy symptoms.

MICROORGANISM—Microscopic plant or animal.

MITES—See Dust mites.

MUCOUS MEMBRANES—Tissues lining nose and respiratory tract; kept moist by mucus.

NEBULIZER—Device used to treat asthma; produces fine mist by passing air through liquid medication; patient inhales mist.

PARADOXICAL BRONCHOCONSTRICTION—Worsening of asthma attack due to overuse of bronchodilators; see Bronchodilators.

PATCH TESTS—Diagnostic test to identify allergens; allergens are applied directly to skin to see if reaction occurs.

PEAK-FLOW METER—Device used to measure air flow in exhaled breath to detect changes in lung function among asthmatics.

PHOTO ALLERGY—Reaction to sun exposure; rare.

PHOTO CONTACT DERMATITIS—Allergic reaction that occurs when a drug or other chemical substance has been ingested and victim is exposed to sunlight; neither chemical nor sunlight alone will cause reaction.

PHOTOTOXICITY—Reaction triggered by exposure to sunlight.

POLLEN—Spores of flowering plants; common allergen.

POLYP—Growth from mucous membrane.

PROVOCATION TEST—Diagnostic test for allergy; involves exposing patient to allergen to see if reaction occurs; see Challenge test.

PRURITUS—Itching.

PSYCHOSOMATIC—Referring to influence of mind on physical well-being.

PULMONARY-FUNCTION TEST—Test of lung efficiency.

RAST—Radioallergosorbent test; measures specific IgE antibodies in blood; can help identify allergen.

REBOUND—Drug response resulting in worsening of symptoms; occurs with overuse of nasal decongestants.

RECEPTORS—Structures on cell surfaces where drugs or chemicals attach or enter.

RETRACTIONS—Chest movements during labored breathing as asthma attack worsens; entire chest area appears to be sucked in with each breath.

RHINITIS—Inflammation of nasal membranes; often due to allergy.

RHINITIS MEDICAMENTOSA—Rhinitis caused by overuse of nasal-decongestant drops and sprays.

SEROUS OTITIS MEDIA—Middle-ear inflammation; seen in children with allergic rhinitis.

SHINERS—See Allergic shiners.

SINUSITIS—Inflammation of sinuses.

SKIN TESTS—Diagnostic tests to identify allergens; involves administering allergens to scratched skin or via injection to see if reaction occurs.

SLOW-REACTING SUBSTANCE OF ANAPHYLAXIS (SRS-A)—Chemicals released by mast cells that set off anaphylactic reaction.

SPINHALER—Device used to administer powdered asthma medication.

SPIROMETER—Device for measuring airway obstruction in asthmatics.

SPORES—Reproductive cells of certain plants; common allergens.

STATUS ASTHMATICUS—Severe asthma attack requiring hospitalization for emergency treatment.

STEROIDS—See Corticosteroids.

SUBCUTANEOUS PROVOCATION AND NEUTRALIZATION—Unproven method of diagnosing and treating allergies; involves injecting suspected allergen under skin.

SUBLINGUAL PROVOCATION AND NEUTRALIZATION—Unproven

method of diagnosing and treating allergies; involves placing suspected allergen under tongue.

THEOPHYLLINE—Most frequently prescribed bronchodilator (see Bronchodilator) for asthma treatment.

URTICARIA—Hives.

WHEAL—Bump in skin; erupts as reaction to allergy test; term also refers to welt that occurs with hives.

WHEEZE—Sound associated with attempt to exhale during asthma attack.

XANTHINES—Bronchodilating drugs for asthma treatment; see Bronchodilators.

ABOUT THE AUTHOR

PAULA DRANOV is a free-lance journalist who often writes about health, fitness and medicine. She has contributed to many national magazines, including *Cosmopolitan, The Ladies' Home Journal, American Health, Savvy, Woman, New York* and *Lear's*. She also has been a Washington correspondent for the Newhouse National News Service covering health and consumer news, and has held various editorial positions with United Press International.